NOTHING
TO HYDE

Sarah

Happy reading

Much happiness

Beryl

aka Claudia .

16th Oct. 2015

DEDICATION

To the memory of all those
mentioned in this book, Mom,
Dad, Nan and especially my dear
brother John who wanted a sister.

Photo front cover by Roy Hipkins.

NOTHING TO HYDE

Growing up in Coseley during the 1930s & 1940s

CLAUDIA HYDE

BREWIN BOOKS

First published by
Brewin Books Ltd, 56 Alcester Road,
Studley, Warwickshire B80 7LG in 2015
www.brewinbooks.com

ISBN: 978-1-85858-546-8

A Cataloguing in Publication Record
for this title is available from the British Library.

Typeset in New Baskerville
Printed in Great Britain by
Hobbs The Printers Ltd.

Contents

Acknowledgements

My grateful thanks to David Edwards who spent hours of his valuable time putting this book on computer. Something I freely admit I couldn't do. Also to my daughter Claudia Zuiderduin who willingly found time to fit the scanning of the pictures into her tight schedule. And to Viv Turner for her encouragement and enthusiasm during the writing of this book. Thanks also go to Alistair Brewin for the art work.

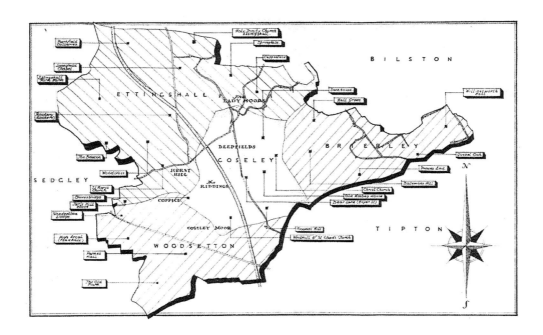

About the Author

Claudia Hyde lives in Coseley in the Black Country and throughout her life has had five different addresses within a half-mile radius. She and her husband have been married for forty-five years. They have a son, daughter and two grandsons.

Twenty-nine years after leaving school she became the founder member of the school's Old Girls' Association.

Since the year 2000 she has produced the Coseley Calendar and in more recent years with her son, using in the main then-and-now pictures with much local history. It is kept by most for reference and sent to many Coseley people who have moved away from the area and to other parts of the world.

Her main interest is genealogy, being a member the Hampshire Genealogical Society, the Hertfordshire Family History Society and The Birmingham and Midland Society for Genealogy and Heraldry which covers the three counties of Staffordshire, Warwickshire and Worcestershire. For nearly twenty years she has been Secretary of the latter's Wolverhampton Branch. Other interests have included philately and collecting photographs of stars of stage, screen and radio. Jazz and blues are her favourite kinds of music, especially traditional jazz closely followed by big band music. Favourite singers Bing Crosby, Frank Sinatra and Johnny Mercer, Doris Day and Ella Fitzgerald. For humour, her favourites are The Two Ronnies, Morecambe and Wise, and the wonderful Hinge and Bracket (George Logan and Patrick Fyffe).

Foreword

Memories are an important aspect of our well-being, a comfort blanket of nostalgic thoughts for the good times, and a lesson to be learnt from the bad.

Each and every one of us has a unique life story to tell, and Claudia Hyde has captured her early years growing up in Coseley in the Black Country with humour, poignancy and the kind of detail that warrants out utmost respect. Depending on our individual age group, there are anecdotes within the story that we can either directly relate to, wonder about, or just simply thoroughly enjoy, and Claudia's memories are able to positively illuminate a period of time that history books tend to describe as dark and forbidding, namely the years that spanned the Second World War.

Every chapter in the book brings its own enchantment, and from beginning to end Claudia's memories are rich, memorable and entertaining.

John Workman
Black Country Bugle

Chapter 1

The light of day first met my eyes on Friday the 10th February 1933 at about 3:15pm. Dad had taken Mom to the Rosemary Ednam Nursing Home, Sedgley for the event which happened quite soon after arriving there. She had refused to leave home until my brother had gone back to school for the afternoon.

John, my brother, had been born about 8:45am on Thursday 2nd June 1927. He was studious and Mom always said he was born in time to go to school and I was born in time to go out. John wanted a sister so he wasn't disappointed.

We lived at 17, Bayer Street, Coseley, (in an area called Roseville) Staffordshire. We being my Dad, Mom, brother, Mom's mother (always called Nan) and me.

The first thing I ever did of note was to climb out of my cot, crawl across the bedroom floor, fall downstairs, crawl across the floor into the front room and climb up onto the couch which was against the wall where the front window was, and this at the age of seventeen months. My Mom, and presumably Nan as well, had left me fast asleep while they went to Roseville Chapel about fifty yards away to pay their last respects at the funeral of Mr. Arthur Nicholls. My Auntie Eva who lived at number 13, by some stroke of good fortune, had seen me and knowing where Mom was,

Bayer Street, looking west. House on left, no.11.

went into the chapel and found her. Auntie told her I was downstairs, was crying and had my head under the curtain. Of course, she rushed home to me and would never forget Arthur Nicholls' funeral.

At less than 2 years of age we moved to 50, Old End Lane to live in a three-bedroomed, double-fronted, semi-detached council house owned by Coseley Council and at the tender age of

Bayer Street, looking east. First house on the right, no.17.

three I had to have five teeth taken out. My Dad took Mom and me in the car to the dentist at Chapel Ash, Wolverhampton. I wanted a cream cake before going in the dentist's but was denied the pleasure as I was due to be given gas. The next thing I remember was waking up on the couch at home with my brother kneeling by me waiting for me to open my eyes.

He said gently, "Hello, who took your teeth out?"

I replied, "Mr. Merry."

John said, "Old merry face," which made me laugh.

The dental practice was Hipkins, Webster, Merry & Moore. What would he have said if I'd been treated by one of the others?

My parents put a wooden gate across the open back door way during good weather. This was supposed to keep me safely indoors which worked except for the time I climbed over it and fell. I still have a tiny scar on my forehead to prove it.

Christmas 1935, Auntie Charlotte and Uncle Will gave me a lovely book called "Just a Funny Book" which used to be read to me. Books are precious and I still have it. One year I had something which wouldn't fit into a bolster slip. It was a desk with a matching chair painted light-green. A few years later, I was given a kaleidoscope which kept me well-occupied, shaking it to change its colourful patterns.

I hated being put to bed and left alone so Mom would sing me to sleep downstairs with, "Daisy, Daisy give me your answer, do."

One night thinking that it had worked, she was carrying me upstairs when I opened my eyes and said, "I'm not asleep, you know."

She took me back downstairs but she must have felt like dropping me. For years I thought an "answer do" was a tangible object. She often said, "Up the wooden hill to Bedfordshire."

As well as "Daisy, Daisy" there was "Little Man You've Had A Busy Day" which I didn't like. It was sad because it was also about the end of the day and I didn't then and still don't like to think of things ending. It made me cry. We had fun when she taught me how to sing a round, and singing, "Row, Row, Row Your Boat."

My cot was wedged between the bedroom wall and Mom's side of the bed. I became very good at climbing over the cot side in the middle of the night, although not fully awake, to snuggle in beside Mom.

I don't remember being in my pram, but I do remember being in my pushchair. On one occasion I'd been taken to Christ Church Summer Fayre held on the cricket field. As Mom pushed me through the gate to come home, heavy rain began to fall accompanied by a thunder storm. We sheltered under the huge pear tree which gave its name to the lane where we were. The tree was removed years ago. The other memory I have of my pushchair was being taken to see Mrs. Fellows, a friend of Mom's. She was the wife of Alan Fellows, who with his brother Bert, owned Fellows's Garage on the corner of Shaw Road with the Birmingham New Road, the A4123. Their house was beside the business premises where Dad used to take the lorries to be serviced. Going to see Mrs. Fellows was fun because her daughter Sheila and I used to play. We were much the same age. She was born July 1932. After the Fellows' business was sold many years later the house, which had been named, "Bowesfield" was demolished to make more room for the subsequent business.

About six miles west of Coseley is Bobbington where Ha'penny Green Airport can be found. Sometimes Dad would drive by the airfield and I always called the billowing windsock, "the things the pigs go in". Perhaps the shape of them made me think of a pig but it always made my family laugh. Being in Ha'penny Green was always a reason for Dad to take advantage of the chance to go to the Royal Oak. Mom and Nan stayed in the car with John and me, and we were treated to pop and crisps.

Shirley Temple, the very pretty child film star, was born in 1928 so was eight in 1936 but I must have been more than three when I was given a glossy book about her called, "Now I am Eight". Oh! to have dimples and curly hair as she did.

When we first moved to Old End Lane, the Silver Jubilee Park was only a thought in the minds of the members of Coseley Council, but by 30th May 1936 it became a fact. It was officially opened by the Chairman of the Council, Cllr. Grange, to commemorate the Silver Jubilee of King George V and Queen Mary. We could see the park from the side of our house.

Mom took me to the clinic in Bayer Street to have an injection, I don't know what it was for, but the place was full of mothers and children, all there for the same reason. Our turn came and I screamed and cried. On the returned visit for the booster, Mom was asked if she would mind waiting until last because I'd upset the other children last time. We waited and went in last and I didn't make a murmur.

Auntie Eva was Mom's sister-in-law, being married to Mom's second brother Albert. They had two sons and lived at 13, Bayer Street. Mom often took me to see her and she would give me a treat of a tiny Hovis loaf which I know cost a penny. One twice the size cost tuppence. Auntie's next-door neighbour was Mrs. Taylor and I liked seeing her. She seemed an old lady but was probably no more than 65. Her daughter, Mrs. Burden, lived next door to her so that took care of numbers 11 and 12.

Years ago there were two theatres in Wolverhampton. The Grand, thankfully, is still there but the Theatre Royal which stood in Queen's Square was demolished many years ago. It was to the Theatre Royal that John and I

On my tricycle age 3, before the Silver Jubilee Park was created.

were taken to the pantomime to see, "Red Riding Hood". We sat near the front row of the Circle. Around the front of the Circle was a ledge covered in red velvet. The ledge was wide enough for the actor playing the wolf to run around. This was exciting for the whole audience. I was probably four years old when I saw this pantomime. The dame who played grandma was good at jumping across her bed to escape the wolf and divesting "herself" of at least a dozen waist slips. Surely money's worth to have remembered it for so long.

The Morgan family lived next door to us at 49, Old End Lane. The daughters were Joan and Jean, both older than me. Joan and Jean were pupils at Dudley Girls' High School, which is no longer there. Sometimes Joan would sit me on her knee and try to get me to pronounce Dudley correctly as I had a problem with the word and instead said Dugley. Occasionally I would stand in the kitchen and watch Mrs. Morgan scrubbing the floor and she would ask me to stand back in case she "spottled" me. The only time I have ever heard that word.

Mr. Morgan had a brother who lived a little way up Castle Street, the main shopping street in Coseley, and no more than two minutes away from where we lived. One day Jean took me to her uncle's cottage and on the way home I fell down and really hurt my left knee. It left another scar which remains to this day.

Dad holding me, with John looking on.

Mom with 6-months-old me, Kinver, 1933.

Another incident involving Jean happened one year on the 11th November. She was selling poppies and had taken me with her. I learnt later it was 11 o'clock, she stood still and silent. I was saying, "Come on", but she wouldn't speak.

After a minute which seemed like an hour she explained what she had done and why. If only she had explained before 11 o'clock.

Nan was a great help to Mom. There were days she would walk me down the lane taking with us a book to read to me whilst sitting on the canal bank and stopping every time we heard a boat coming so that we could watch the horses pulling the boats. Sometimes she would take me in the opposite direction crossing over the Birmingham New Road and walking up Mason Street and turning right walking to the top of Hospital Lane and into the uneven fields, the area known as the Brampits, where we would sit and I'd be read to. The one day I remember so clearly was when poor Nan lost the back door key and we had to wait for Mom to return from wherever she'd been. It was only a short wait. Nan went back to look for it, but the key was never found.

Auntie Charlotte was the wife of Mom's eldest brother Will. They had two daughters, my cousins Joan and Vera who were both older that me. Mom took me quite often to visit her sister-in-law. The house where they lived in Harding Street had a downstairs bathroom and during one visit I needed to go to the bathroom and forgetting that Bob, their black Spaniel dog, had been shut in there to keep him safely away from us, I opened the door and within seconds his teeth were sunk into my right upper arm. Out came the iodine and the dog was suitably chastised.

Before I started school and later during school holidays, Mom would give me a treat by taking me through Roseville to the Clayton Playing Fields to play on the swings, slide, roundabout and rocking horse, all there for the younger children. I wasn't allowed in the sand pit as Mom didn't consider it clean enough. All these were on what was called the little side. Similar things were over the far side of the field for those eleven and over and was called, "the big side".

I was taught by my brother how to tell the time. Using a dinner plate he drew round it on a piece of cardboard, cut out the circle, drew on the numbers and fixed the cut-out fingers in the centre with a paper fastener and we were ready for lessons.

John made a chair for me out of a box which he had broken up. We were outside in the back yard and when it was finished he proudly picked me up and sat me on it. It's a good job he was there to catch me when the chair collapsed.

Dad had been born in Kinver and spent the first five or six years of his life there. Most weekends he would take us to Kinver Edge going through Enville for us to go on the Common.

One Sunday we saw Brenda Mead and her parents there. They kept a shop along the Birmingham New Road. All my memories are clear but one is indescribably vivid. Dad and I were on our own and it must have been a weekday. I was sitting in the front passenger seat and as we were going through Enville on the road alongside the Common, Dad suddenly stopped the car with the urgent instruction to stay where I was. He quickly got out of the car and I became aware of him killing with a stick a snake which he had seen crossing the road. Having lived in Kinver he was probably aware that if anyone had been bitten, it would have been serious. It was almost certainly an adder.

St. Chad's Church was near to home and could be seen with its recognisable spire on the hill, the far side of the park from our side gate. This was the church that Mom and Nan went to, and so did I at the age of 5. It took a quarter of an hour to reach it with my little legs. Most Sundays Mom went to the 8am Holy Communion service, but when she went at 11 o'clock, I went with her. I loved the incense and it was just part of my religious upbringing. It wasn't used at Christ Church where Mom had previously attended and had done so since her

St Chad's Church, from the park.

Christ Church, Coseley.

childhood, but when we moved to Old End Lane, St. Chad's was so much nearer. She knew a lady named Mrs. Jevon (Nelly) whose husband Joe was in the choir. They and their son Derek, the same age as my brother, walked up all the way from Barnsley Road, a road off Higgins Avenue. Barnsley Road no longer exists. Mom used to watch for Mrs. Jevon who would take me to church with her. When I was old enough I would go first into Sunday School. I knew several little girls near to my age who lived in Vicarage Road. Two sisters from one family went to Roseville Methodist Chapel and three sisters from another family attended Ebenezer Baptist Chapel. Three other girls went to St. Chad's. They were Mary Clarke and Ann Phipps who were cousins and the third one was Mary Banks. She and I were separated in age by just one week, she having been born on the 3rd February in the same nursing home and our mothers were in the beds next to each other. Mothers and babies were kept in for two weeks.

1937 and Walt Disney made his first full-length film, "Snow White and the Seven Dwarfs". Eventually it came to The New Theatre Royal in Wolverhampton and Mom took a very excited me to see the cartoon masterpiece. We watched entranced until I began to cry uncontrollably. No! It wasn't when the wicked

On the left: 49 and 50, Old End Lane, looking down Vicarage Road.

queen poisoned the apple to give to Snow White, and it wasn't when Snow White was in the glass coffin. Mom found out when she rushed me into the foyer that it was when Snow White sang, "Some day my Prince will come". I realised that if he did come she would go to the castle with him so I told Mom, "I don't want Snow White to leave the dwarves". My ever quick-thinking mother said, "She won't leave them. She'll take them with her to live in the castle". So, well pacified, we went back in to see what remained of the film.

My Dad, Claud Wallace Hyde, ran a haulage contracting business with his brother Harry. The business was called

Mom by VP8936.

9

Left: Wal. Hyde Bros. Their Leyland lorry. Right: Dad with driver, Len Brant and his mate on the lorry.

Wal. Hyde Brothers although Dad was the younger brother. They shared a car, a Standard Ten, which was how we managed to get out into the country. The car was grey and the numberplate was BOM 82. We had one holiday in Rhyl when I was very small but by the time I was five the Standard was replaced with a beautiful dark blue Wolseley 14 with blue leather upholstery. Its number was FOE 594. In 1938 we went on holiday to Weymouth and for this there was a very good reason. Dad's Auntie Gertie, my grandfather's only sister, lived in Weymouth. This was because her father had been an official at Portland Prison before retiring to Weymouth. My great-grandfather died in 1905 at the age of sixty. She no longer lived in the house where they had lived together and hadn't done so for many years. In fact, when she was eight in 1877, her mother had died at the early age of 27, leaving her husband with little Gertie, her two older brothers Vivian and Alfred (my grandfather), and a younger brother Harry. Taking advice from his mother-in-law, he advertised for a live-in housekeeper/nurse maid whom he could trust to be a surrogate mother to his precious children now that he no longer had his darling

Bertha. After several interviews, he gave the position to one Sarah Ansell. As well as board and lodging, she was given £15 a year. This lady moved with the family because of grandfather's job, from London to Leeds, then Rochester and lastly Portland. When grandfather died, Auntie Gertie and Miss Ansell set up in business together running a boarding house overlooking the sea where they mainly accommodated the wives of navel officers who came to see their husbands when their ships were in dock in Portland and Weymouth. When Miss Ansell died in 1921, Gertie carried on alone in her grief until she retired and moved to 70, Dorchester Road which was a very large semi-detached house which had been made into flats and she occupied the one downstairs. Auntie was 59 when we went there in 1938.

On the steps of 70, Dorchester Road, Weymouth, with Auntie Gertie.

On the way to Weymouth Dad wound down the car window and, being a man of few words, asked a man, "The way to Frome?"! The snappy retort came back, "Froom, Froom". (So that's how it's pronounced!)

Auntie spoke beautifully and thinking my manner of speaking was not good enough I asked, "May I have that maid of honour plarze?" My poor parents were so embarrassed.

We stayed at a flat over a shop in Abbotsbury Road. When Dad had taken the cases upstairs he walked down to the seafront and booked a place on a fishing boat for the next morning. This was so that he might catch some mackerel for the next day as we were self-catering. The shop owners had a cat named Dinkie and I used to shake up the cushion on the chair he was used to and call to him, "Come on Dinkie, your cushion's ready," and he'd come running.

Every morning John and I were taken on the sands and like so many other children took our buckets and spades and made sand castles. We enjoyed paddling, but most of all we looked forward to our daily donkey rides. The donkeys had their

Left: On the donkeys, Weymouth 1938. Right: John, Dad, Auntie Gertie and Nan with little me on Chesil Beach, 1938.

names on their bridles and I always wanted to ride on Mike. The Donkey man sang "South of the Border" all the time as if it was the only song he knew. The Punch and Judy show was always exciting but Weymouth beach had something special. There was a man who was a sand artist and he built perfect replicas of cathedrals in the sand. We saw auntie most afternoons and Dad enjoyed taking us to Osmington Mills for the special treat of a lobster tea. Another day we went, taking auntie with us, to Portland Bill, an area which had been home to her for some years. Mom's camera was rarely out of her hands at this time as she loved to have a photographic record not only of holidays but also around home and the local area. On this day, we stopped at Chesil Beach and as ever there are photos to prove it. Dad persuaded Mom that a day trip to France was a good idea so he booked the tickets and off we went to Cherbourg. We didn't have long there, but we did go to a restaurant where Mom had junket (very French) which she didn't like. When we sailed for home we stood on deck waving to lots of people waving goodbye to us. On the Saturday, we said our farewells to auntie and Dad brought us home.

Apart from Uncle Will and Uncle Albert, my Mom had had another brother. He was John and had died of pneumonia at the age of 23 in 1923.

Dad had two brothers apart from Uncle Harry. They were Grandma and Grandad's eldest and youngest sons, both dying when babies, George in 1897 and Cyril in 1907.

Uncle Albert and Auntie Eva's two sons were William (Bill) and Albert, usually referred to as "young Albert" but later in life known as Bob. They were separated in age by five years. Both of them passed the scholarship when in the top class of Mount Pleasant Junior School and went to Wolverhampton Grammar School. When Bill left school, having applied to the G.P.O. for a job, he was called to London for interview. This meant a train journey and not only did Auntie Eva go with him but also Mom and me. I don't know exactly where the interview was held but the job was to do with telecommunications. The only memory I have of that day is walking along a footpath with iron railings outside the houses and small flowers growing between them. We were only away from home for one day. Bill did get the job.

How well I remember Mrs. Morgan from next door coming in and saying she'd give me sixpence if I'd drink the glass of milk I'd previously said I didn't want. This was too good a chance to miss.

I said, "Just for drinking that?"

She said, "Yes." So I drank it.

What I didn't know until later was that it had caster oil well blended in it to treat my stubborn tummy.

It was September 1938 and my cousins Dorothy and Rita and I had been asked to be bridesmaids at a relative's wedding at St. Chad's Church. The three dresses were the same style with a double frill around the hem. The other two dresses were pink but mine was blue as was that of the chief bridesmaid. She was grown up so it was a different style. Don't believe the saying, "Three times a bridesmaid never a bride". I was a bridesmaid three more times after this.

John and I had lovely Christmases. The real tree would arrive in the house and after being put into a large pot of soil, out would come the decorations which had been in their box since the previous Christmas and several before. I enjoyed putting little bits of cotton wool (snow) on the tips of the boughs. The living room was always decorated with paper streamers, bells and balls.

We had a couple of years being given Rupert Annuals, then at Christmas 1938 there was the Film Fun Annual. This was for John, but I had years of pleasure from it. In 2010 I managed to get a copy of this on eBay. I usually had a doll. One year John had a piano accordion which he knew he was having as Dad bought it from his cousin Harold in Stourbridge, but John knew he couldn't have it until Christmas. Naturally, he woke everyone up playing it at about 3am. Everyone, that is, except me, as I was already with John looking at what Father Christmas had brought. I had lovely story books but I also enjoyed my post office set and my John Bull printing outfit with its backward letters. Then one year my presents were not in a pillow slip but a bolster slip and at the bottom in the corner and the last thing to come out was a little box. I opened it to find a small expandable silver bracelet.

John and I were encouraged to read so when I was very small, Mom bought me "Tiny Tots" a children's comic long defunct. It contained a picture colouring competition which I once won. I was sent a postcard-sized certificate on which it said that I'd been awarded the Tiny Tots Order of Merit and could write T.T.O.M. after my name. So young, I took this seriously and wrote it after my name in all my books. At least I'd done something to make Mom and Dad pleased with me. The card was framed and hung on the wall beside the fireplace. John had the Hotspur and Film Fun.

Around this time, Mom and Nan listened to two particular radio programmes. "In Town Tonight" was a topical programme and "Monday Night at Eight" an entertainment programme, a mixture of music and comedy. My introduction to Arthur Askey, Richard Murdoch and the "The Bee Song" and my love of radio.

Chapter 2

My hair was light brown and straight, parted on the left with a bow of ribbon on the right side and this is how I looked when I started school at Mount Pleasant after the Easter holidays in 1938. My first teacher was Miss Sneyd. Mr. George Stanley Grange, known by some parents as "Stan" as he was a Coseley man and he himself had attended Mount Pleasant School, had been made Headmaster of the Infants and Junior School. Mom knew Mr. Grange, as she too had attended Mount Pleasant. Miss Sneyd lived in "York House", the very last house in Coseley on the left before crossing from Coseley into Wolverhampton at Parkfield. In 1966 the Coseley boundary with Wolverhampton was changed.

The first thing I learnt when I started school was where the toilets were. "Inside the school", you would think. No such luck.

"Please Miss, may I leave the room?" ensured a walk across the playground to an isolated block out of sight of any of the school windows, although we could wash our hands in the cloakroom back in school.

Something we had at break every day was milk. A bottle of ⅓ of a pint. It was years before I realised why it didn't taste the same as that we sometimes had in bottles at home. School milk was Grade A and at home we had sterilised which I much preferred. For a long time I wondered why the milk was called "grey day". During the Winter when the milk at school was very cold, the bottles were put

Mount Pleasant School Caretaker's house, in the school grounds.

Mount Pleasant Street.

to stand on the hot water pipes around the walls of the classroom. The classrooms were heated by these pipes which in turn were heated by the coke fire in the stoke hole underneath part of the school. This was attended to by the caretaker Mr. Grove who with his wife and family lived in the caretaker's house in the school grounds.

In the same class with me was Sheila Boucker, Olive Osborne and my little friend Mary Banks, all of whom lived in Vicarage Road and Derek Rhodes who lived only two doors away from me at number 48. It was when Mary was only five that her mother died and before long Mary's grandmother, her mother's mother Mrs. Cadd, gave up her home somewhere in the country and came to look after Mary and Mr. Banks.

Walking to school, being taken by Mom, we passed a low wall where elderly men gathered to sit and chat. The one often had with him the tiniest dog imaginable. I used to ask him, "Have you got Queenie with you?" and he'd reply, "I'll have a look". He'd put his hand in his jacket pocket and fetch out a little scrap of canine beauty. I don't know who the man was, but I believe he lived in Wallbrook. It was he who said he'd give me a little pot. It was a three-legged cast-iron pot covered with orange-coloured enamel with the word "CANNON"

Left: Claudia Beryl Hyde, age 6 months. August 1933. Right: John Alfred Hyde, age 6 months. December 1927.

embossed on it and had a brass handle. Most likely a traveller's sample made years before Uncle Albert was made foreman of the Cannon enamelling shop.

During my first year at school I had made friends with a very nice little girl named Marjorie Smout. It shocked everyone when Marjorie suddenly died. I remember clearly how she used to knit scarves for her dolls. She was the daughter of my Dad's friend Horace Smout who was the local coal merchant whose house and business was in Ebenezer Street.

Every so often, Mom would book the chimney sweep to come to clean the living room chimney. There was rarely a fire lit in the sitting room. I don't know the name of the man who came, but he was uncle to Muriel Brookes who was in the same class as me. She lived in Fullwoods End with her parents and sister Freda and her uncle lived next door to them.

The daily newspaper carried the edition number on the front page every day. Mom used to cut out these numbers and stick them onto a card until she had enough to send for the items which were on offer. Usually this meant books, Mom ever ready to supplement our education. One which we had was called "Children's Everything Within" and was about three inches thick. It touched on so many subjects including Morse code and semaphore. I loved that book. We also had a pair of encyclopædias.

It was in one of these I was looking through with Dad when I saw a picture of something I didn't recognise so I asked, "What's that Dad?"

He answered, "That's television. It is about being able to watch moving pictures at home."

I said, "Can we have one?"

He said, "No. We'll never be able to afford one of those." This was in 1938.

Around this time Dad changed the radiogram for a console radio which stood on the floor. Dad bought a new separate HMV record player, and the records were mostly 6d. each from Woolworths. Now I had a new interest. I would sit on the floor with my ear very near to the radio loudspeaker and listen to all the dance music programmes that I could. Jack Payne, Henry Hall, Jack Hylton, Ted Heath and anyone else who was on offer.

We didn't have fitted carpets at home so the floor was covered with lino and rugs. The lino had worn so Mom ordered some more from Kirklands in Bilston. The son of the firm, Sid Kirkland, came to fit it on the floor. It was Summer and a very hot day. I was about five at this time and as I stood watching Mr. Kirkland sweating with the effort of cutting and laying the lino I was overcome with pity and picked up the skirt of my little dress and put it over his head to wipe his forehead. His remark was, in a true Black Country accent, "Yaow waow duw that wen yaowm abeut aiteen."

Dad was insured with a company who employed two brothers. I think they lived in Penn. They were Vic and Cyril Lloyd. One of them didn't have any children and he teased me by asking me to go and live with him and his wife.

I said, "I'll come if my Mommy can come."

He said, "I don't want your Mommy as well."

They laughed at the joke. The other Mr. Lloyd used to press Mom, a non-smoker, to accept a cigarette which would stay on the shelf above the fire place for weeks. Dad hadn't smoked cigarettes since I was very small. He had become a pipe smoker and on a shelf in the pantry was a tin with packs of Digger and Erinmore tobacco.

The Rickward family lived next door at 1, Vicarage Road. Mrs. Rickward senior, her son Herbert and his wife Sally. They had had a son named Harold in June 1937. He was left with his grandma one day when his mother went to a cinema in Wolverhampton to see Fredric March and Janet Gaynor in "A Star Is Born" taking me with her.

There was a small cinema in Ivyhouse Lane owned by Mr. Page. It was just known as Page's. The building is still there but is now used by the British Legion. It is now known as the Coseley Ex-Servicemen's Club & Institute.

The time was nearing when we wouldn't need to go to Wolverhampton nor Dudley to go to a palatial cinema because diagonally across the road from our house had stood a large house called Old End Hall, behind a high wall. Both house and wall were being taken down and replaced by a beautiful cinema to be called the Clifton. My Dad made friends with the works manager named Mr. Mitchell. He and his wife

Mrs. Rickward, my cousin Rita, I'm holding Harold Rickward whilst George Jeavons looks on.

On the front lawn, showing how near we lived to the Clifton. FOE 594 is parked in Mason street as there was nowhere else to park it and very little traffic at the time.

had three daughters and the family lived in a house along the Birmingham New Road just past Fellow's Garage. The youngest daughter Barbara was my age, her two older sisters were Gladys and Joan. The family originally lived in Lancashire. Once or twice we were invited to their house for tea. Before the cinema was officially opened, Dad and I were taken by Mr. Mitchell to the projection room and I saw a row of six different coloured leavers which represented different lights which when operated appeared to change the colour of the ruched curtains which covered the screen during the interval. The Clifton was built to seat 1004. It was officially opened on Saturday 8th July 1939 and Dad had managed to get tickets for the special occasion so Mom, Dad, Nan, John and I went. During the proceedings I whispered to Mom that I wanted to go to the toilet. I knew where it was so I was allowed to go on my own. Eventually she realised I'd been away longer than necessary so she came to find me calling my name and getting a tearful reply. The fresh paint on the door had caused it to stick so Mom went off to get help and back came a man with a screwdriver and took off the door. There was no gap top nor bottom of the door so she'd been unable to pass me a hankie to wipe my eyes. It was a frightening experience for a six-year-old.

The staff of the Clifton wore green and gold uniforms. The ladies in green dresses with large gold bows across the front and the commissionaire, Mr. Stanford, wore a full-length green coat and peaked cap both decorated with gold braid and buttons. They were very smart as was the manager, Mr. Crane, who always wore a dinner jacket and black bow tie. The Clifton was a most impressive building announcing CLIFTON in very large red, neon letters high up on the building and could be seen from a long distance.

Most people like ice cream and none more so than children, that's why we used to watch for the ice cream man. He didn't come driving a van, but riding a bike with a large container on the front. A penny for a single cone and 2d. for a double. If we had a double we could have vanilla in one side and strawberry in the other. The manufacturer was Eldorado.

Mom and Nan were on the rota for cleaning the brasses at St. Chad's Church and on one of the walls in the sacristy were photographs of the vicars who had held office there. Nan pointed out Father Charles de Renzi who had been the first vicar and said, "He married me". I never knew my Grandad as he died in 1914 and not understanding my Nan I thought the late vicar was my Grandad. Nan told me on one occasion that when she was a little girl she used to stand and watch the church being built. It was consecrated on Wednesday 28th March, 1883; but it did not become a separate parish until Monday 14th April 1884. The Foundation stone was laid on St. Chad's Day 2nd March 1882. Nan and Grandad (Clara Smith and Thomas Newton) were married there on 2nd October 1892.

In the border on the edge of the lawn, Dad grew alyssum, lobelia, thrift, Carnations and antirrhinums which we always called snapdragons. Alongside the house was a trellis on which grew Alexandra Roses. Nothing which took a lot of cultivating, just weeding and watering when necessary.

Clara Newton.

The Newton Family. Left to right: William, Clara with John, Thomas with their son Albert.

Mom and Dad's wedding picture. Left to right: Amy White, Isaac Gorton, Emily
Gorton, Beatrice Newton, Albert Newton, Mary (Polly) Newton, Clara Newton, John
Alfred Coles Hyde, William Newton, Charlotte Newton, seated: Victoria Barrett, Emily
Newton Hyde, Best Man: Harry Alfred Hyde, Wal. Hyde, Eva Newton holding baby
Albert (later called, "Bob"), seated at the front: Ida Newton and William Newton.

Dad liked to have a walk on Sunday nights and often took me with him. When the carnations were out in the garden he would pick one for his buttonhole and off we'd go, usually as far as the traffic lights at The Foxyards. He loved me to wear my white dress, red blazer, white socks and black patent leather shoes. Mom told me years later that when I was six months old she wanted to enter me in a baby competition but Dad said no because he knew I was the best. One day Dad took me for a walk through Swan Village and up towards Mons Hill. We walked along a narrow path on the side of the hill. The right side as we walked was wooded as the left side was open and we could see for miles. We soon came to an isolated old house and just passed it was a large deep hole with four sloping sides which met at the bottom almost to a point. I was scared of falling in. We didn't walk home that way. One Sunday we had quite an adventure when Dad and Mom took

John and me walking up Brook Street when we were caught in a shower but this wasn't rain, it was a shower of tiny frogs, each about the size of an adult's thumbnail. It was amazing and how it could be no one has ever been able to explain.

Just down from Brook Street the same road becomes Bourne Street and on a different occasion Dad and I were walking there when we came upon berries growing in the hedgerow and Dad stopped and drew my attention to them and said, "Don't ever eat any of those. They're called Deadly Nightshade."

We went again to Weymouth to see Auntie Gertie in 1939. We called to see her on our way to our digs. This time we didn't have a flat but as last time we stayed in Abbotsbury Road. The house was owned and run by Mrs. Strickland so this time Mom did no cooking. We went again to Osmington Mills for a lobster tea. One day we went to Lulworth Cove and another to Portland

Victoria Barrett and Emily Newton, dressed for their parts in a play at Christ Church, about 1916.

taking Auntie with us of course. Our day trip this year was to the Isle of Wight. On the ship on the way there I made friends with twin girls about my age. They were named Sylvia and Joy and were absolutely nothing alike. Mom took a photo of Dad on the front at Cowes as he stood by the small cannons which stretch there for a distance. Most days we fed the swans on Radipole Lake. John and I were taken one evening to the cinema to see the film "Gunga Din" which made an impression on me. We went to see Auntie Gertie before setting off for home. On the journey home Dad said to Mom, "You know Em, I don't think we shall see Auntie again."

This was the last holiday we were to have together.

On Sunday 3rd September 1939 war was declared between Great Britain (France, New Zealand and Australia) and Germany and things were never to be the same again.

In the same year, on the 31st October, Uncle Harry's wife, Auntie Tory (actually Victoria Alexandra), gave birth to their son Gordon. A brother for 10½ year-old Rita and the last cousin that John and I were to have.

Auntie Tory and Mom had been best friends from school days and both attending Christ Church every Sunday. They were both only daughters and in the mid-1920s married the Hyde brothers becoming very close sisters-in-law.

The gas street lights were no longer lit each evening and turned off every morning by Mr. Charlie Townley who we were used to seeing on his bike balancing his ladder, the tool of his trade, over his shoulder. The big red letters on the Clifton would not be seen again until the end of the war whenever that might be and who would win? We didn't know.

Chapter 3

In Miss Sneyd's class we started to learn to read and write although I could write my name before I started school. The desks were painted yellow. They were each made with bench seats to accommodate two pupils.

We had all now moved up to Miss Pearson's class which was a little more advanced.

Our desks in this class were the same type as in Miss Sneyd's but this time they were painted green. They were arranged two deep against three walls of the classroom. When Miss Pearson was ready to finish teaching each afternoon, she asked us to stand and would say, "Hands together, eyes closed", and she would say a prayer to which we would conclude, "Amen", never knowing that Eric Pepper who sat behind me was pushing me in the back with the tips of his middle fingers.

When the Morgan family moved to a large detached private house at the top of Coppice Road, Mr. Morgan's sister, husband and little son George came to live at 49. He was younger than me but we were good playmates. George's grandmother Mrs. Morgan Snr. lived with her daughter and son-in-law and always wore an ankle-length black dress.

Quite soon after war broke out, every house was issued with an Anderson air raid shelter made of corrugated iron and as our backyard joined with that of next door, Mr. Jeavons and Dad dug out the required-sized hole and built the shelter joining the two together so when there was an air raid

John with Jean Morgan and Molly.

warning, both families went down the shelter in the dark until the all-clear sounded. Mrs. Morgan Snr. was a dear old lady. She used to make Mom and Nan laugh when she'd try to tell them about people she knew but couldn't remember their names.

She'd say, "You know whossit, lives up whereisit in them houses?"

If she heard an aeroplane, she'd say, "Hark! Hush! Listen! 'E's either gooin' or cummin' back."

She was a lady who I learnt later in life had lost two sons in the First World War. I have a memory of seeing her placing flowers at the foot of the tree near the park gate on the corner of Mason Street with the Birmingham New Road which was dedicated to the memory of one of her sons. This tree was one of about 350 stretching along the Birmingham New Road running through Coseley from Parkfield Road on the Wolverhampton border to the Dudley border, each tree in memory of a Coseley service man who had lost his life in the First World War.

We at school had air raid practice. This involved walking in an orderly fashion to the brick-built shelter which was on the opposite side of Ivyhouse Lane and down the path. The building was on the left. Apart from the shelter there was nothing but open fields. The shelter and the fields are no longer there, the land is presently covered by houses where Berrington Drive is now. The shelter was never used for its intended purpose. The air raids in this area were all at night.

By this time in the war, everyone in the country had been issued with a gas mask with instructions to carry it everywhere they went. This was in case of gas attacks by enemy aircraft. If we forgot to take it to school, we were sent back home to get it. We were strictly forbidden to put the gas mask on the floor under the desk and use it as a foot rest.

Something else everyone had was an identification number. Mine was ORLC 272/4. The head of the family was given the number ending with 1 and so on down to the youngest. We also had identification cards.

At this time in history, as well as London, many other cities and towns were being bombed by the German Luftwaffe. On the night of 30th August at 9.30pm, a bomb fell on the "Horse & Jockey" in Ivyhouse Lane. The pub had in recent years been built to replace the old pub and because the excessively strong pitch pine timber had been used in the roof, the bomb rested there and exploded

The Horse & Jockey where the bomb fell on the night of 30th August 1940.

upwards. Amazingly, no one was killed, but the blast from the explosion affected lots of buildings locally. This affected my Great Aunt Adeline, Nan's sister, who lived in Ward Street. A few nights later, a landmine fell at the bottom of Bradley's Lane, very near to the G.W.R. Railway line which no longer exists.

It was in 1941, April I believe, that one of the bombs that was dropped on Weymouth ruined Auntie Gertie's lovely flat and she was bombed out. She had difficulty in finding other accommodation. Eventually, her new address was 2 Lennox Street. It was a holiday boarding house and all she could have was one room. During the Summer Season, she was required to move upstairs to the top floor to a smaller room, taking all her belongings with her. She was able to move to the original room at the end of the season. She loved her personal belongings and was a hoarder, so everything like photographs and family papers were kept in a trunk. Her furniture was put into storage in anticipation of finding another flat, but try as she might, this never happened and she passed away after a few weeks' illness in a Nursing Home in November 1967, aged 98.

We had a budgie and when it died it was put into a tin and buried by Dad in the small piece of garden which connected with that of number 49. Soon after, we asked if we could have another, so along came a large aviary with two rooms which accommodated at least ten budgies. I didn't know what Dad's idea was. If

Our wire-haired fox terriers, Spot and Frisky.

it was to breed them it never happened. The aviary was raised up at each corner on two bricks and when the birds threw their eggs out of the nesting boxes, Dad realised there were rats under the aviary so the budgies went (I know not where) and the rats as well.

Dad was always fair and when John asked if we could have a dog, of course we had two. They were wire-haired fox terriers, bred by Mr. Percy Bartley who lived down Old End Lane. John's was given the name Spot. He was smaller than mine which was named Frisky. It wasn't long before it was discovered that Frisky was subjected to fits so he was taken back to Mr. Bartley. We had Spot until 1948.

Next to St. Chad's Infants School was the Church Army building. Connected to St. Chad's Church was Captain Barstow. He lived with his wife and family in a house at the top of Mason Street. St. Chad's had no church hall at this time and the Church Army building was used as a social club as well as a venue for concerts and plays. I well remember Mrs. Clarke singing "Smiling Through" at one concert and Reg Smart playing the part of a character called Garth. So convincing was he that for years I thought it was his real name. A year or two into the war the use of the building totally changed. All over the country, places were opened called British Restaurants where cheap nutritious meals could be bought which helped supplement rations. Lots of them stayed in use for a few years after the war. They were then called Civic Restaurants. Neither the Church Army building nor the Infants' School are still there.

Still on the subject of food, our green groceries were bought from Mr. Birchall. His shop was in High Street, Tipton but he came around in his lorry which was really a travelling shop. One of his stops was outside our front gate where several customers gathered knowing what time he was due. There was a drain in the gutter nearby and one day when Mr. Birchall and his son Sidney came, a half-crown was dropped. I don't know who dropped it. I only know it rolled down the drain.

In the greenhouse on the park, tomatoes were grown by the park keeper Mr. Balshaw and when they were in season the word went around and people queued at the park keeper's house where each person was allowed two tomatoes. A similar thing happened when the sausage arrived at the butcher's.

There have always been local singers and concerts to entertain the populace and Coseley wasn't short of talent. Mom took me to a concert at the Mary Dermott Memorial Hall in Gough Road where I heard a lady named Joan Lamb sing. She had a beautiful soprano voice. On another occasion we went to Darkhouse Baptist but the concert must have been in the long-gone Sunday School building which was on the opposite side of the road from the chapel. It was there that I heard Fred Pardoe singing the funny song, "The Bold Gendarmes", otherwise known as "We'll Run Them In". I must have been all of 4 years old then, but I only have to hear it and I think of Fred.

I must have been about 7 when I was given a new doll's pram. It really was lovely and would have held a newborn baby. I had had a doll's pram for several years, a much

Mom and me with Spot on the lawn at 50, Old End Lane.

smaller one. Mom said she knew a lady in Providence Row who wanted it for her little girl so one day we pushed it to the lady's house and to its new owner Irene Smallman. Soon after this I went to play with Isabel Greensill and saw she had a doll's pram exactly like mine.

Since the Clifton cinema had been opened, Dad had taken to seeing every film that came. On Mondays and Thursdays he would go to the Clifton and before long he started taking me with him. We sat downstairs at the cost of 1/3d. for Dad and 10d. for me. Eventually the price went up to 1/6d. and still it was 10d. for me. He always said I'd got to choose which night I was going. I'd say Monday but when Thursday came I'd beg to go again and usually did. He always listened to the headlines on the 6 o'clock news on the radio before leaving home, then one night, downstairs was full, so Dad for the first time went upstairs at a cost of 1/9d. and still 10d. for me. The seats where we sat became our regular seats as the ones downstairs had been our regular ones.

Uncle Will came most Sunday mornings to see his mother and sister, after singing in the choir at Christ Church. He would sit reading the newspaper he'd bought at Elwell's in Tunnel Street.

One day I looked at his hands holding his paper and was startled by what I saw but said nothing until he'd left.

John and me in the park, with Spot.

Then I asked, "Mom, what's the matter with Uncle Will's hand?"

She told me, "He lost all the fingers on his left hand in an accident at work."

When I was older she added to the story, telling me that he had worked at The Cannon Iron Foundries for only two weeks at the age of 14 when the accident happened. He could no longer do that job but was told he would have a job at The Cannon for the rest of his life in the time office but he never had any compensation. My cousin Bob told me that at the beginning of WW1 when they went round recruiting men to join the army, Uncle Will held up his left hand and said, "I'll come if you think I can fire a gun with this." No more was said.

Cousin Bob was always an extrovert and one day Mom called us to the window to see him. He was rounding the far corner of the Clifton. What a sight: he was walking on stilts. He came like that all the way from 25, Langley Avenue.

Chapter 4

Miss Stant taught the 7-year olds and now I was in her class. The desks weren't painted: just ordinary dark wood. There were more children in this class as several had moved to Mount Pleasant School from the infants' schools of St. Chad's and Christ Church. These schools were at opposite ends of Coseley and the children had a distance to walk. It was at this time that I met Eileen Armstrong who was to become my life-long friend. There was a girl in our class named Kathleen Baldwin who was an evacuee and came from Balham, London. I have no idea who she lived with nor where she lived, unlike Eileen and Pat Taylor who had moved up from Gillingham in Kent to live with their grandparents in Mount Pleasant Street.

During the war there were occasionally weeks specially given over to raise funds to help the war effort. One year, there was War Weapons Week and another Spitfire Week when we could buy a badge with a Spitfire aeroplane engraved on it for 6d.

We were encouraged to take money to school every Monday to buy saving stamps. When we had saved enough sixpenny stamps, 30, we could exchange them for a 15/-, (fifteen shillings) War Saving Certificate which was stuck in a blue covered certificate book. These stamps and certificates were not just available at school but anyone could save this way by buying them from the Post Office.

At the age of about seven I had my first pair of glasses. I don't know

Taken from the National Savings Certificates book.

why I had to wear them but after a second pair, my eye problem was obviously corrected. I had to visit the Eye Infirmary in Wolverhampton on one occasion during this time and the eye drops made my eyes so blurred, I was afraid and thought I'd never see properly again. My brother always wore glasses and at times I would go to the Eye Infirmary with him and Mom when she took him to see Miss Voysey, then to the optician, Brian P. Birmingham in Chapel Ash to get new glasses.

One day, my ever-vigilant mother, asked me to close my teeth together and show her. This I did and to her horror, she could see what she suspected that my bottom teeth overlapped the top ones. This meant an urgent visit to Hipkins, Webster, Merry and Moore, where my mouth was closely inspected by which one of the quartet, I don't know, but he certainly knew how to correct my problem. All my bottom teeth had to be totally encased in silver-coloured metal. Mom asked how long it would have to stay on and she was told it might be three months or it might be three years. I was a source of entertainment to my classmates who wanted to look at my bottom "teeth". I was taken back to the dentist three months later. He prised the metal away from my teeth in pieces. It was good to know the problem had been corrected and I would not have a protruding jaw.

When the register was called in Miss Stant's class, we had to answer with the number we had each been given. Robert Addiss was "one": I was forty-two, the class being called in alphabetical order. There were about 50 in the class.

Sometimes when Miss Stant had finished her lesson before the bell went to indicate time to go home, she would say, "Arthur Webb, come and tell us a story", and we'd be treated to a "Just William" story, the telling of which would have delighted the author Richmal Crompton herself. Another day she would say, "Barry Lane, come and recite a poem", and we'd be entertained with Barry's rendition of "Albert and the Lion". We didn't need Stanley Holloway when we had Barry.

Our council house had previously been the home of Mr. and Mrs. Hoggins. He was the Relieving Officer for Coseley and managed the Relieving Office, a small building in Groucutt Street. The rent of our council house was 10/- a week. The smaller houses in Vicarage Road were 8/6d. Mr. Deakin was the rent collector and he called for the money every Monday morning and signed the rent book. He lived in the Parkes Hall area and so did his granddaughter Maisie Deakin whom I knew at school.

Our house did have a bathroom but none of the council houses had indoor toilets. They were in semi-detached buildings at the back of the houses, so the toilet for number 50 was attached to that of 49. Our toilet had another use; it housed a small step ladder, a long-handled lawnmower and a clothes horse which came out every week so that the freshly-ironed washing could be hung on it and aired. It was my regular job to fold the no-longer-needed daily newspaper into neat squares, carefully cut with a knife, and string them up to be hung in the toilet.

Years into the future 50, 49, 48 and 47 Old End Lane lost their identity to 2, 4, 6 and 8 Central Drive respectively, when that road was cut straight through to link up with Fountain Lane.

We always called Dad's mother "Grandma". She lived at the back of and over the shop, in which Grandad had installed their daughter, my Auntie Maud who had been trained as a milliner but by the time I knew the shop, it was a sweets and tobacconist. The shop was in Castle Street, number 36 and next to the "Apple Tree" pub. I used to go to see Grandma going in through the shop, telling Auntie I was just going to see Grandma. It was no use going until after

Castle Street, Coseley. Auntie Maud's shop was no. 36.

midday, as she was a very late riser. In the small room behind the shop the only heat she had was the tiniest gas fire on top of which was usually a very small saucepan with cocoa in it. She never drank tea or coffee, something she hadn't drunk, so I was told years later was something to do with one of her pregnancies of which she'd had five. Sometimes Grandma's sister Lilian came over from Stourbridge for a day or two and when I knew she was there I would hurry up to the shop to see her. She fascinated me because she smoked. I'd never seen a woman smoke before. Grandma had her radio on all the time. It ran on an accumulator which had to be charged up in a special way. One place where this could be done was Dave Millard's. It was an ironmonger's shop and to get there one had to walk along Castle Street to The Square then down Tunnel Street to Fullwoods End where the shop was. It usually fell to the lot of Auntie Maud's daughter, my cousin Dorothy, to take back the accumulator but I remember once doing this myself. Going to Castle Street could sometimes be dangerous and scary. In the village there was a butcher named Sid Guest who had his own milking cows. They grazed in a field on the opposite side of Old End Lane from where we lived. Between home and the corner of Canal Street there was a high

This picture shows the curve in Old End Lane, and on the left where Sid Guest grazed his cows. The foreground is now where The Apple Tree pub is situated. Photograph taken by Harry Preston.

wall which surrounded Mr. Guest's pig yard and occasionally I got caught between home and Grandma's when the cows had been milked in the milking parlour in the yard behind the butcher's shop and the herd was returning to the field. I would flatten myself against the wall, scared of being hurt by them, especially as they had horns.

The cows were followed by Sid Meese, stick in hand, to keep them in order. It was these same cows that provided the milk we had daily delivered to the door by Mr. Meese. He came in a horse-drawn cart which carried churns of milk. On the sides of the churns were hung pint and half-pint and gill measuring cans used to fill the customers' jugs with the required amount.

Whenever Dad felt he had a cold coming, he would ask Mom, "Em, get me some quinine". He firmly believed this would prevent it from developing. This meant a visit to Mr. Marsh Fellows' shop. Once when I went there with Mom, he asked me my name, so I told him my second name, the one I was used to: Beryl. He asked me if I knew it was in the Bible. I didn't, and nor did Mom. He quoted chapter and verse, so at home Mom looked it up. Book of Revelation chapter 21, verse 20, and as Mr. Fellows had said, beryl is a precious stone. On another occasion, Mom sent me to the chemist to fetch some juniper pills. Afraid of forgetting the word I'd never heard before, I chanted it to myself all the way there.

Another "first" for me was the day I was in Jevon Street and saw Miss Nicholls driving a car obviously on her way to "Alpha House", Avenue Road, to her job as she was the dispenser for Dr. Waddell and Dr. Kemp. At this time, she made up all prescriptions for the practice. I knew she did this but I didn't know ladies drove cars.

During the war, all food was on ration and everyone had to be registered with a grocer and a butcher who would cut out the relevant coupons from the ration books. We were registered with Joseph Smith who had a family-run grocer's shop in Castle Street. His wife, their two sons Gilbert and Neville and their respective wives Ivy and Mary, also worked in the shop. Our butcher was the second shop owned by Mr. Udall and run by Mr. Bill Reynolds. This shop was also in Castle Street. Our potato peelings were saved and every few days, Mom and I walked to Vicarage Road West where the two Miss Sheldons lived with their brothers. They kept fowl and were grateful for the peelings which they cooked to make food for them. In return, Mom was able to buy a few eggs. These helped to supplement the rations.

Auntie Gertie had given Mom a beautiful pottery basket in yellow with decoration of forget-me-nots. It stood on the front window ledge. Mom had gone shopping in Wolverhampton and John and I were watching for her coming home. When we saw her, I excitedly knocked the ornament off the window ledge and of course it was broken. I cried, and John said he'd go and meet her, ever my protector, and tell her what I'd done. She was very upset, and mended it with Certofix as best she could. It was given a new home on the piano.

Dad and uncle transported Hercules cycles (in pieces and packed in wooden boxes) to Liverpool docks, and once Dad took me.

I remember being taken through the Mersey Tunnel. On one occasion, Dad told Auntie Gertie how wonderful the tunnel was, and that it was lined with black glass. Not understanding, she said, "With what Wally?"

So Dad repeated, "Black glass."

After some moments' thought, she said, "Oh! You mean black glarse."

Chapter 5

At school, Miss Flavell had the 8-year-old pupils. Hanging on the wall in her classroom was a mirror, too high for us to look into. The frame was like a lifebelt and written around were the words AM I CLEAN AND TIDY. It was in her class that I learnt that H.C.F. was the highest common factor and L.C.M. was the lowest common multiple, whatever good that has done me, but during good weather, she would take us out into the playground along with a wind-up gramophone, and we would march around in formation. Most enjoyable. What we called sums I didn't find easy. Mom put me through my paces teaching me and testing me on mathematical tables, but for some reason, I had trouble remembering the answer to 7x6 and Mom would ask it every so often until I answered 42 every time without trouble. Mr. Grange took assembly most mornings at school. We always had a psalm and although there are 150 of them, we only ever sang the 23rd or the 150th.

There were two incidents which involved being visited by the doctor after having childhood ailments. The first was when Dr. Waddell came to see me. I was on the mend, and he must have thought I'd be even better for a dose of fresh air.

So he said, "Put her coat on and I'll take her on my rounds with me."

So off we went, driving up towards Sedgley. His first stop was at a large house at the top of Sedgley Hill (Tipton Road) where he called to see his first patient and as far as I was concerned, his last. I didn't like sitting in his car on my own.

When he came back I tearfully said, "I want to go back to my Mommy." To avoid the flood gates opening, he took me home.

The second incident was when Dr. Kemp, who was in the same practice with Dr. Waddell, came. I'd been ill in bed again, and presumably had lost my appetite and had remembered hearing what was an old song, "A Little of What You Fancy Does You Good".

I asked him, "Doctor, can I have a little of what I fancy?"

He asked me, "What do you fancy?"

I answered, "Gray peas and steamed fish." (Not together of course).

Doctor said, "Yes."

Mom said that it was obvious I didn't want anything greasy. I wasn't allowed to forget what I'd said.

My spelling was as bad as my arithmetic, so Uncle Albert called me Little Alfie after a cartoon character in one of the newspapers who also had problems with spelling. Uncle's first name was Thomas so to tease him, I called him Tommy. With this in mind, when my next birthday came around, he wrote on his card to me, "Alfie, a little of what you fancy – gray peas and steamed fish, Tommy". It became a standing joke and I still have that birthday card.

My brother had been having piano lessons for some time with Mr. Gill who lived in Princes End and I wanted to have lessons as well. John used to take me sometimes on the crossbar of his bike going down Old End Lane over the canal and railway bridges and coming out into Fountain Lane and down into Princes End. I took the first playing and theory exams and passed, and that was as far as it went, but John was excellent. He practised which was something I didn't like to do. (In years to come he obtained a Bachelor of Music degree at Birmingham University). When he took exams, Mom, Nan, John and I used to go by bus to Birmingham sitting upstairs on the long front seat if we possibly could, and enjoying the long journey. I always looked to see a large detached house in its own grounds at Oldbury. Its name was Edale which could clearly be seen spelled out in large capital letters in concrete slabs set in the sloping lawn. Sadly it is no longer there, but replaced by a restaurant. After John's exams at the Queen's Hotel, our treat was to stand outside the sweet shop in Broad Street and watch the toffee-blending machine pulling and twisting the toffee around and around. John always passed his exams and several times was awarded with a medal.

St. Chad's Church magazine was a monthly publication and Mom was one of the distributors, delivering them to customers in Old End Lane, Wilson Road and Vicarage Road. This was how I came to know some of the older ladies in the community. Not as old as Mrs. Poyner and Mrs. Porter, was Mrs. Millinson and when she had her third daughter Christine, Mom sent me down to Mrs. Millinson to give her a jar of Horlicks and to see the baby of course.

Weaver's Bakery and the day with Joan was a one-off experience. Dad had a friend named Len Weaver who owned a bakery at the back of his house in Clifton Street, Hurst Hill. He had a daughter named Joan who was about the same age as me. Mr. Weaver and Dad arranged for me to go and play with her one day during the school holidays. It wasn't long before we were in the bakery where I was fascinated, watching the baker kneading the dough and putting it into the bread tins. Using both hands, he took the same amount of dough in each, rolled each handful into a ball and set them side by side into a tin to make a 2 lb (2 pound) loaf, the type that could be torn apart and sold as half a loaf, if necessary. Naturally, I wanted to try my hand at rolling the dough and putting the two handfuls in a tin. It looked so easy watching this professional, moulding dough and baking a perfect loaf. I had visions of taking a loaf of delicious bread home. When it came out of the oven, it hadn't risen, but I took it home with pride. Dad collected me and I told him all about the bread and showed it to him. Mom cut into it and to my horror, it was a shocking shade of grey, but I think my dear parents pretended it was the ultimate in bread. At this time in history, due to the war, butter was on ration, each person getting only 2 oz (2 ounces) a week. If we spread butter on our bread, we weren't allowed jam. Only if we spread margarine on our bread, would Mom allow us to cover it with jam. The taste of the war-time margarine was horrible. I was about eight when this happened.

Mary Banks, me, Emily Hyde, John Hyde and Bob Newton, taking Spot for a walk after meeting Mary and me out of Sunday School and picking bluebells from the vicarage garden, c. 1941.

By this time, I knew what I wanted to do when I grew up: to work in a shoe shop and sell only high heels or to be a lift attendant. I did neither. Life has enough ups and downs.

I was suitably chastised one Sunday morning when Father Bourne could no longer stand my incessant talking. He turned around from the altar and called out my name. He told my mother about this so I was told off again.

At Easter 1942, I was given a white hymn and prayer book (Hymns Ancient & Modern and The Book of Common Prayer – many years later I carried this book at my wedding, and not a bouquet). The price is still on its box: 10/- (ten shillings).

In Coseley, there was a coach (or as we then called the vehicles, "char-a-bancs") proprietor named Len Barnett. He lived in Old End Lane but he kept his coaches in a very large garage in School Street. This was very convenient when it came to Sunday School treats. Two of these occasions I remember very clearly. The first was when I was about seven and our outing was to Clent Hills only about ten miles away and just over the South Staffordshire border into Worcestershire which was very handy, as with the war on, petrol was rationed. Our mothers were allowed to go with us. There were donkey rides to be had which was exciting as I hadn't seen a donkey since our last Weymouth holiday. Mom said I could have a donkey ride, so I was helped up onto the animal's back, and we set off in single file along a narrow path. On the right side of the path was a thorn hedge which very soon badly scratched my little leg, and looking down I saw blood running down into my white sock and I could do nothing to stop it. The second outing was to Sutton Park in Sutton Coldfield years later in 1946. On this occasion I was with Jane Tapsell. It was there that we met three Roman Catholic lads on an outing with their priest. One of the lads and I exchanged addresses and we corresponded for years even when he went into the army.

Unimaginable today to realise that Roseville had a very nice hat shop. It was owned by Mrs. Bates. During the Summer months, she had a lovely selection of straw bonnets which fastened with a ribbon bow under the chin for us girls. We had straw hats as we grew older, but it was lovely to be dressed properly. Straw bonnets were strictly for Sunday best.

Father Bourne, the vicar of St. Chad's church, was quite a character. He was a tall man who rode his large bicycle everywhere. One day, dressed as always in his black suit, "dog collar" and wide-brimmed trilby, he was riding through Roseville when a lad called after him, "Destry rides again". Continuing to ride, he turned towards the direction of the voice and his authoritative voice simply said, "Vulgar boy".

"Destry Rides Again" was a 1939 cowboy film about a law-abiding mild-mannered sheriff who gets mad at local corruption, a starring role for James Stewart.

Invited to preach on a special occasion at Christ Church, a glass of water had been placed on the edge of the pulpit for Father Bourne, but in his enthusiasm he sent the full glass flying.

There was one day during the war when something exciting happened. I don't expect it matters now after so many years, but Dad came home carrying a suitcase. It was full of tins of food of varying kinds. Some had the labels partly burnt and others with the labels totally burnt off.

Mom would sometimes say, "Shall we have a mystery tin?"

We didn't know if we'd have meat or fruit. It appeared there had been a fire at a warehouse somewhere and somehow Dad had come by the tins. No questions asked.

Next door to Uncle Albert and Auntie Eva in Langley Avenue, lived Welsh Mr and Mrs. Williams and their daughter Myfanwy. One day, when visiting Auntie Eva, I went in to see Mrs. Williams and she asked if I wanted a piece of the cake she'd made. Of course, I said, "Yes please."

One taste and I said, "I'm sorry, I don't like it."

It was caraway seed cake. I'd never had any before and I haven't had any since. This goes in the same category as coffee, of which I've had a lifelong dislike.

The solicitor which Dad and Uncle used was Foley Eggington in Sutton Coldfield. There was a day when Dad had to visit the solicitor and he took me with him for the ride. Once there, I sat in the car waiting for him, looking at the trees and fields, so the place must have been on the edge of the town.

I had a pack of playing cards with pictures of Walt Disney characters on them. Ordinary card games could be played with them because of there being fifty-two cards in four sets, but instead of hearts, clubs, diamonds, spades, these cards were in four sets with either a black, green, blue or yellow spot in the corners.

When Uncle Albert visited us, he often played cards with me. Nan used to play with me using a pack of ordinary cards and I would say such things as, "Play your king, Nan", or "Play your ace". This went on for some time and she would ask how I knew what she held. After weeks and weeks, I confessed I could see their reflection in her glasses.

Chapter 6

At Mount Pleasant School, Mrs. Jones had the next class I was in. She was a Welsh lady. There were two teachers who didn't seem to have their own classes, but taught girls from other teachers' classes once a week. Mrs. Fellows took us for needlework: embroidery and sewing. I can hear her now saying when she was pleased by something a pupil had made, "That's a lovely little garment". Miss Taylor taught us knitting. We were knitting dishcloths in some thick string-like stuff which I couldn't do without getting holes in it because I could never remember which hand the thread should be in if I'd put the knitting down and picked it up again.

One day, Miss Taylor was so cross with me when I asked for help, she snatched it from me and said, "Oh! Give it to Pearl White". A very nice girl and prize knitter.

We sometimes went to Tipton Baths and our mothers were allowed to go with us. The swimming instructress could see I was hopeless after a couple of lessons but I was glad because I hated it. There has been a Coseley Swimming Baths built since then and sadly demolished in March 2010.

At about this time, a boy in my class named Joseph Mason, who lived in Old End Lane, died as the result of an accident. He died towards the end of 1943. Six of us from the class were chosen to go to the funeral at Old Meeting chapel. It was very sad as he was an only child. His cousin Derek Rhodes was in the same class. He lived next door but one to me at number 48. He too was an only child. We sometimes played together and I enjoyed going to see his Mom.

One day a handsome army officer in full uniform walked through the school hall heading for the Headmaster's room. He was 2nd Lieutenant Douglas Baker, who later rose to the rank of Lieutenant. He was a teacher at Mount Pleasant School in peacetime.

All schools go through phases of playing different games at playtime and one of these crazes was to do handstands, or as we called it, toss up, against the school wall. Every playtime we tucked our skirts into the elastic of the legs of our knickers and tried to do handstands. Sylvia Jones was brilliant at this but I was hopeless. At home, I told Dad about it.

He said, "I can do that."

So we went out onto the backyard where Dad proved he was as good as his word. Dad, never a man to use a purse, had his change tumbling out of his trouser pocket. I started picking it up, then Dad soon came down.

He said, "Come on you little madam, give it to me." It was fun.

Another friend was June Cooper, and like me, she enjoyed going to the Clifton. One morning, she couldn't wait to ask me if I'd been to see "Now, Voyager". I hadn't then, but that evening Dad and I went to see it. Bette Davis, Claude Rains and Paul Henreid at their best. Quite often Grandma went to the Clifton and if I was there I'd know where to find her. She'd be sitting in the end seat of the third row from the back. There was a good reason for this. On the metal upright on the side of the seat, there was an electric socket where she could plug in the hearing aid which she would get from the box office when she bought her ticket. With this she could hear the film perfectly. I once asked her who her favourite film star was and without hesitation she said, "James Cagney".

An extraordinary thing happened one day when I was walking down the bottom of Vicarage Road with Mom. We met a lady pushing a pram and Mom asked the lady if I could look at her baby, as she had the same name as me: Beryl Hyde. I actually recognised the lady as she was an usherette at the Clifton. I think I was about nine or ten when this happened. This lady must have known my cousin Arthur Sheward as he was a commissionaire at the Clifton and there he met Doris Lowe who also was an usherette. They were married on 29th May 1944. Arthur was the eldest son of Auntie Maud and Uncle Ernie. Their two younger sons were Alfred and George being Dorothy's three brothers.

Thanks to Mom letting me have the postage stamps, I was able to indulge in the hobby of collecting signed photographs of stars of stage, screen and radio, by writing to them at film studios in this country and America, the BBC and Wolverhampton Grand Theatre and Dudley Hippodrome from where I had that of Laurel and Hardy. It was easy to post my letters as the letter box was attached to the gas lamp on the corner of Old End Lane and Castle Street. We could always see the postman come to collect the letters.

The film book which Mary Banks sometimes lent to me was no longer available on the last occasion when I asked to borrow it. She said she'd given it away. I had had so much pleasure from that book. Eventually, I found out she'd given it to Doreen Clamp, so Mary had the last laugh if indeed that was what she wanted. Another book borrowed from Mary was about famous women. It was from that, that I first learnt about Emmeline Pankhurst, Grace Darling, Florence Nightingale and Madame Curie. Mary did upset me once to the extent that I told Mom that I didn't care because she would die a week before me. Mom said that life didn't work like that. Mary became a librarian in Coseley Library. She and I didn't often fall out. In fact when it was bluebell time in Spring, Fr. Bourne gave us permission to pick them out of the vicarage garden where there was a huge bed of them and we did this together when we came out of Sunday school. After Mary married and went to live in Cheshire, we remained friends and corresponded until she passed away in 1992.

It was getting near to the last Sunday in April which was the annual day of Roseville Methodist Chapel Anniversary. Sheila and her sister Beryl had been practising their hymns for weeks, ready to go on the platform and sing word perfect for God and the congregation. I finally persuaded Mom to take me to see my friends in their white dresses on the platform. We were Anglican and didn't have an anniversary but instead had a Sunday-school festival. We did wear white dresses and white veils as well. We stood in the choir stalls to sing, not facing the congregation and every year amongst other music sang Jerusalem. In chapel, the raised platform faced the congregation and one hymn I have never forgotten were words set to Dvořák's Humoresque in G Flat Major. All the chapels of every denomination sold Phul-Nana sent cards for a penny, each advertising the anniversary and times of services. On these occasions there were also street processions when half-a-dozen or so adults would carry collecting tins to collect money from passers-by and those who were standing on their doorsteps having come out to see the parade.

Some Sundays I went to Evensong with Mom and on one occasion I remember so well we walked home with Mr and Mrs. Flavell who were our near neighbours. Mom walked with Leah and Wal and I went ahead, turned into the park before them and when they caught us up we were standing looking out towards Great Barr and counting barrage balloons. They were large hydrogen gas-filled balloons which were fastened in some way to the ground. They were in defence of the country against The German Luftwaffe who were coming over regularly at this time to bomb the area. We counted about a hundred balloons that night.

Names fascinated me from an early age and when about nine I asked Mom what Nan's name was before she was married and she told me Smith. I asked what Grandma's name was before she was married and was told Mobberley. Then I asked if I hadn't been given my name what might it have been and she said they'd thought about Patricia and Doris then decided on Claudia Beryl. Then she said they later thought I could have been Lucia after Dad's ship H.M.S. Lucia but I'm happy with the names they chose. Mom had a friend named Dorothy Jones whose daughter was Beryl who had a cousin named Claudia and deciding they liked both of these, it was perfect with Dad's first name being Claud. Enquiring further, I asked what name I would have had if I'd been a boy and she said that it would have been Geoffrey. I would have been pleased with that. I said, "When I grow up, I'm going to have a boy and a girl and call them John and Claudia". Well, I did.

Apparently, Dad should have been Wallace Claud, but Grandad said he didn't want him to have the initials W.C. (for obvious reasons), so that's why he was Claud Wallace.

Grandad Hyde, named John Alfred Coles (his mother's maiden name being Coles), was always known as Alf. He was the only one of his siblings to leave the family home and move to the Black Country. This was because of his work as he was a Customs and Excise Officer. His job took him to many local pubs where the beer was brewed by the licensee so he had to test it to make sure it was up to the correct standard for sale. It was called measuring the gravity of the beer. One pub he went to was "The Five Ways" at Cradley Heath. There he met Florence Louisa Mobberley, the daughter of Samuel Mobberley the licensee and his wife Elizabeth née Attwood. When they eventually moved to Coseley, Grandad became the Captain of Coseley Second XI cricket team.

Grandad's own paternal grandfather was John Hyde. He was born in Hertfordshire and married Eliza Young who lived in the same county. They soon went to live in Windsor where John became a groomsman at Windsor Castle and some years later moved to Buckingham Palace.

Grandad Newton was named Thomas, the same as his father, and was a file cutter who worked at the little workshop along the path called, "The File Cutters", which ran between Church Road and Summerhill Road. His father originally came from Birmingham but his work on the canal boats brought him through Coseley where he met Hannah (the daughter of Arthur Wise and Sarah née Bullock) as Arthur was the canal toll house keeper at Deepfields, Coseley. Sarah originally came from Wednesbury.

Nan was Clara Smith and her family home was in Mason Street, Coseley, where she lived with her parents Isaac and Esther née Fownes. (One relative spelt his name without the "w"). Isaac was a whitesmith and Esther made nails in the backyard. It had been suggested that Clara should carry on at school and become an uncertificated teacher, but her parents could not afford to let this happen, so she went into service at "The Spread Eagle" in Church Road a mile away from Mason Street. This being near to where Thomas worked, and his home on The Paddock is, no doubt, how they met.

Nan was one of a family of eleven children – she, her sisters and brothers who still lived locally. My Great-Uncle Tom and his wife lived in Pool Street in the Parkes Hall area of Coseley, not very far from two of their daughters Maude and Elsie. Always called Auntie Maud, was Mrs. Rudd. She had a daughter, my second cousin, Pauline who was about eighteen months older than me. We used to play together when the grown-up chat was going on. Pauline had a two-wheel bike which she had outgrown, so it was decided that Dad should buy it for me. So I had Pauline's three-quarter-size bike and she had a full-size one. I couldn't ride a two-wheel bike, so my cousin Albert, who in later years and explanations later, would answer only to the name Bob, taught me to ride on our partly-curved front lawn by holding the back of the saddle. Thinking he was running behind me, I was surprised as I curved round and saw him standing watching me. I could ride! Pauline later had a sister named Jennifer and again later a brother named Stuart.

Something I played with a lot was a cut-out book. On the cardboard cover had been four grown-up girls. Two on the back and two on the front. I'd cut them out carefully as I did with the dresses and hats on the pages inside and it was so interesting dressing the cut-out girls in the different paper clothes.

The Hyde Family, 1909.

John was very artistic and he made pictures on glass using embroidery transfers and pretty silver paper. The background of the pictures were usually painted black so the coloured designs or figures stood out beautifully. He framed them using passe-partout. This had to be bought from a shop in Wolverhampton called Start's in Victoria Street. He made a pair with an 18th century lady and gentleman on them which he gave to Mrs. Rickward and for as long as she lived there they hung on her front room wall.

On one of my trips into the country, we collected fir cones, the biggest and best we could find, and I painted them using art paint making them to hang on the Christmas tree.

Christmas was upon us again, and I was given by my parents two story books, "The Abbey Ruins", and "Mulberry Hall" by Joan Fleming. These books were different, not necessarily because the stories were very exciting, but because they were printed on dark grey paper. At this time there was a shortage of paper. I had never before, nor have I since, seen books like these. I still have them.

Along the Birmingham New Road, opposite Ebenezer Baptist Chapel was a very large advertising hoarding. The only one that ever made any impact on me had on it:

Three words to the WHOLE NATION

GO TO IT!

Herbert Morrison

I didn't understand it at the time as I was too young, but they were meant to be words of encouragement to the population to do what they could for the war effort. Herbert Morrison was the Home Secretary in the wartime coalition Government.

During the war, lots of people voluntarily "did their bit" on the home front. Dad was in the A.R.P. (Air Raid Precautions) later called the Civil Defence. It was they who helped distribute the Anderson and Morrison shelters to every house in the country and they were trained to be of help to people should they be bombed-out or split-up from members of their families. At night, they patrolled the street, looking to see if any light could be seen where curtains didn't meet. If this happened, the householder would be told, as even small lights could

Birmingham New Road, Coseley. On the extreme left, where the Herbert Morrison poster was.

be seen from the air. Mom was embarrassed one night when an air-raid warden knocked the door to tell her there was a light showing.

The air-raid post was a small brick building where the A.R.P. members were stationed. This was next to a large wooden building which was the British Legion, otherwise called the Ex-Servicemen's club in Bank Street. Some householders were issued with stirrup pumps in case of fires and they were given black cards with a big white S.P. on them to let people know where they could get a stirrup pump if necessary. There was one at our house. The difference between an Anderson shelter like the one we had and a Morrison shelter was the latter was inside the person's house.

Mom and Nan knitted socks and gloves for the armed forces in khaki, navy blue and air force blue with whichever colour wool was brought to them by Mrs. Waddell the doctor's wife. She and Mom were in the W.V.S. (Women's Voluntary Service), now W.R.V.S. She always admired their knitting and said no one could turn a heel as good as Mom and Nan. Mom also joined the First Aid and went to classes at Bayer Street Clinic. From Mom's book, I learnt the circulation of the blood and recited it for Mrs. Waddell. Uncle Harry became a Special Constable.

Dad was born in December 1899 and at the tender age of 15 ran away from home to join the Army. He'd probably seen the poster showing General Kitchener saying, "Your Country Needs You", and taken it seriously but no matter, his Mom and Dad fetched him home but not before he'd been kitted out with full uniform and had a photograph taken in it. At this time he was under age but in 1917 the First World War was still raging so he joined the Navy and after his training in Portsmouth was assigned to H.M.S. Lucia, a supply ship going at some stage through the Baltic Sea to Finland and Russia. Uncle Harry was already in the Navy serving on H.M.S. Cardiff.

On leave at the same time, they had their photograph taken together in uniform. Dad must have been one of the very few who were in the Army AND the Navy at some time between 1914 and 1918.

Dad in the army, age 15.

Dad with his brother, Harry, 1918.

At this time the Hyde family home was 8 Railway Terrace which stood on land now covered by Willowfields retirement flats.

Scarlet fever was a disease that didn't miss me. It was April 1943 and because I had a brother who could have caught it from me, I was taken to Moxley Isolation Hospital in Bull Lane. It had two large wards separated by a long path covered overhead to protect walkers from inclement weather. The one ward was for scarlet fever patients and the other was the diphtheria ward.

The sweet ration limited us to 2 oz (ounces) a week for children and adults alike and Mom used to bring my ration, and possibly her own, to the gatehouse for me. Mrs. Sayce and her daughter lived there and they brought everything up for the patients as we weren't allowed visitors. We were made to take a spoonful of cod liver oil every

Dad, seated, with unnamed friend.

day, and to help the medicine go down, I cut my Mars bars into slices and immediately had one after the dreaded oil. Mom also sent me writing paper and stamps so that I could write home which I did almost every day using an indelible pencil (no Biro pens then). I've never forgotten the name of the boy in a bed diagonally opposite mine. He was Harmon Finkelstein and was about thirteen years old. There was a Swiss nurse named Trudy Reichland and a Hungarian nurse taught me the alphabet of the British sign language for the deaf. She also gave me a couple of Hungarian stamps for my collection. They were probably pre-war as post from Hungary would have been impossible at that time. I wasn't the only Coseley child with scarlet fever as Dorothy Evans was in there too. In one of Mom's letters, she told me that Mrs. Rickward had had a baby girl, so I sent a list of girls names to her, writing the names of all the girls I knew, and that was how Joan got her name. After three weeks, my parents were told they could fetch me home. When they came, Mom came up to the window behind my bed all smiles, then saw I was crying.

I said, "I can't come home?"

She found out from Matron Curtin that I had a diphtheria germ and had to be kept in until I was free of it. I was in fact a carrier. I was taken along the path to the diphtheria ward during which time, swabs were taken regularly from my nose and throat. Three negative results had to be achieved consecutively, but they kept proving positive, positive, then a negative then back to a positive, and it was five weeks before three negative swabs were taken. One night during this time, I crept out of my bed to go to the bathroom and I pinched my finger between the nail and knuckle so badly that it broke the skin and bled profusely. I cried silently with difficulty because I didn't want to wake up the other patients but oh! the blood on the white counterpane! Before I went into Moxley, I didn't like cabbage nor white of egg, but when I left there I could happily eat both and I'd also learnt how to do "hospital corners" when making a bed. Dad and Mom fetched me after nine weeks away from home. The ceilings in the hospital were so high, an optical illusion caused me to think our bedroom ceilings had been lowered. As if! I had graduated from reading "Tiny Tots", so now Mom bought Enid Blyton's "Sunny Stories" every fortnight while I was away. It had been a weekly publication but with the paper shortage during the war, it was now only every two weeks. My little paperbacks were waiting for me in a neat pile on the front room window ledge. Mom had taught me how to mix mustard powder with milk and a pinch of salt and I learnt later that Dad had said he wouldn't have any more until his little girl came home to make it for him.

Whilst I was in Moxley Isolation Hospital I met a girl named Vera Cole, who was a few years older than me. She lived in Mount Road, Lanesfield, an area of Coseley. As Mom used to visit Mr. Lewis a chiropodist whose surgery was at his home in Mount Road, I used to go with her and take the opportunity to visit Vera. Her dad kept pigeons and one day he gave me a pigeon's egg which Mom boiled for me as she would a hen's egg. It tasted the same, but what was expected to be white was opaque.

Sometimes at school, the pupils from the top class would put on a concert for the rest of the school. I was impressed by Norma Cooper, June's big sister, wearing a long dress, open parasol resting on her shoulder and her rendition of "Little Old Lady (Passing By)".

In 1943 there was a grand garden fête on August Bank Holiday Monday in the grounds of Himley Hall. At that time, bank holiday was the first Monday in

August, not the last as it is today (it became statutory in 1971, following a trial period from 1965 to 1970). It was held in aid of the Red Cross and the war effort in general. Dad took us as a family to this great event. We walked around the grounds visiting all the stalls. When I noticed a tennis racket (second-hand, of course) I asked Dad to buy it for me. He did. It cost the princely sum of ten shillings. I imagined being able to play when I grew up. I never did, and anyone less interested in sport would be difficult to find.

Even when we'd lived in Bayer Street there had been a telephone in the house for Dad and Uncle's haulage business. The number was Sedgley 131. The number went with us to Old End Lane and a few years later it was changed to Sedgley 2131. I must have been about ten when a telephone engineer came to the house and took out the ordinary 'phone and installed a small switchboard. The calls for the Coseley Welding Company came through on our 'phone and the switchboard had two extensions, one to the office which was in the grounds of the factory and one to Uncle Harry's house which meant that Mom could 'phone the required extension by holding down the appropriate key and turning the handle on the side of the switchboard. Neighbours used to come to the house if they needed to make urgent calls such as doctors or hospitals as the nearest telephone box was next to the Birmingham New Road on the ground now covered by Jack Newell Court. One neighbour came to ring a distant hospital so many times that I still remember its number: Chaddesley Corbett 240. At this time, it wasn't possible to dial direct with an S.T.D. (Subscriber Trunk Dialling) code as it is today. That development came many years later.

Chapter 7

Mr. Hopton was the teacher of the top class of the Junior School. A tall thin man with a moustache and straight black hair who did not believe in sparing the rod. I once counted how many times I could recall being given the cane, usually across the tips of the fingers on my left hand: thirteen times. I expect I'd been talking but I think he loved that cane.

Occasionally, when Mr. Hopton was out of the classroom, the Headmaster, Mr. Grange, would come in to give us a lesson. One day, he wrote on the blackboard:

OREYVA OBZORQ YNFG AVTUG

and asked if anyone knew what it meant. No one did and he said it was a code and a simple one at that. He explained, by writing all the letters A to M and underneath them the letters N to Z and transferring the letters, you would read "Berlin bombed last night". Like this:

A B C D E F G H I J K L M
N O P Q R S T U V W X Y Z

B E R L I N   B O M B E D   L A S T   N I G H T
O R E Y V A   O B Z O R Q   Y N F G   A V T U G

I was fascinated as I'd never heard of codes before. In years to come, I went to Bletchley Park, base of the code breakers in the Second World War.

Decades later, I came to know Mr. and Mrs. Grange socially, and he asked me to call him Stan. I said I couldn't as he was my Headmaster. "Yes," he said "but I'm not now."

From then on, he was Stan and his wife was Linda. By this time, Mom had passed away and one day he told me he remembered my mother from when he

Left: Mount Pleasant School showing the stoke hole, bottom right of picture, shortly before the sad demise of this building. Right: George Stanley Grange, Headmaster of Mount Pleasant Junior School from 1938 until his retirement in 1968.

was a young man and he said she was the most beautiful girl in Coseley. I felt so proud of the compliment he'd paid her and looking at her photographs, I can easily believe it. On a different occasion, I asked him if he remembered giving me the cane one morning for being late? He said he didn't, but I assured him he did. He was a grand man.

Mount Pleasant Infants' and Junior School on the right, The Cookery Centre on the left.

Roseville Chapel had a youth club and sometimes I went with Sheila Boucker. I knew most of the children who went there but most of all, I remember Linda Bayliss who sang beautifully and every time I went, I asked her to sing, "The Fishermen of England" for me, and she did.

Quite often, Mom visited her aunt, her father's sister Elizabeth, who lived at 35 Havacre Lane. Sometimes, we walked through Roseville to get there or go a different way which took us along the Birmingham New Road, cutting across the fields and over the canal bridge. The Coseley School now covers this land. This route took us past some private semi-detached houses which back in 1932 Dad had suggested to Mom that they might buy one.

Elizabeth Newton Price, "Aunt Bet".

35, Havacre Lane, the centre of the three buildings.

Her response was, "No, we'd never be able to afford it". They were new then, and cost £250.

The house where Aunt Bet lived was the quaintest two-roomed cottage imaginable. It had no gas nor electricity. All the cooking was done on the range where the fire not only heated the room, but also cooked the food in the oven at the side of the fire. When it was dark, the cottage was lit by an oil lamp. Out through the back door and along a short passage, there was first a wash house then a toilet. The main railway line ran very near to the boundary of the property.

Aunt Bet was never short of ginger biscuits. She was of that generation of ladies who never wore skirts above their ankles and what's more, they always seemed to be black. She was born in February 1865 and in her late teens went to America working in the cotton fields in the Deep South as a missionary. She was a very strong Baptist. In October 1899, she married a man named Charles Springer and they lived in Coatesville, Pennsylvania. Their son Ebenezer Newton Springer was born on 22nd July the following year and died on the same day. Three months later she noted in her little book "Dear Charlie Springer killed while in discharge of his duty on the W. & N.R.R. Company at Coatesville 18th October, 1900."

Sisters Elizabeth Price and Mary Newton (my great-aunts, Bet and Polly) outside 35, Havacre Lane.

Eventually she married again. He was another Charles, surnamed Price. His occupation is unknown, but he was a prison visitor. The story goes that he was still alive when Aunt Bet came back to England to escape him. This may or may not be true.

Her oldest sister Mary, better known as Auntie Polly, had shared the cottage with her until her sudden death in October 1935. She never married and her work had taken her up north where she had been a companion/housekeeper to Deaconess Haig in Gateshead-on-Tyne. On the way back from what was always called "the cot" (short for "the cottage"), if I was in luck, we'd stop at Round's

Left: Tunnel Street from The Square. Right: Tunnel Street in the process of demolition, looking towards The Square.

cake shop in Tunnel Street. Served by Charlie Round's daughter, Leila. I'd always choose a gorgeous macaroon which I called half chocolate and half plain. The unusual thing was they were baked on melt-in-the-mouth rice paper. When Aunt Bet died in August 1943 (aged 78) it was left to Mom and her cousin to clear out "the cot". I used to go with Mom, and Ida brought her daughter Glennis with her who at that time was half my age. In years to come, we met up again as a result of a request for her whereabouts in the Express & Star.

Although there were only two rooms in "the cot", there were a lot of belongings to be sorted out, which took at least a week.

Often, I'd been told by Mom about her Uncle Isaac. He'd been married to her father's sister, Emily, but she had died in 1927. In September 1931 he married his niece Rose. She was the daughter of yet another of Mom's father's sisters, Esther. She was much younger than Isaac and hadn't been married before. Isaac and Emily had had no family so there were no children involved. At this time, it was against the law for a man to marry his wife's sister's daughter. One day I was playing hopscotch on the footpath on the opposite side of the road, when Mom called me. She had a gentleman with her and she seemed very excited.

I went over to her and she asked, "Do you know who this is?" Without hesitation I said, "Uncle Isaac". Mom was so pleased to see him after such a long time.

He and Aunt Rose lived in Lichfield. He asked Mom and Dad if they would allow me to go and stay with them. He asked a second cousin of mine, whom I didn't know, to go as well. She was named Gwen and was engaged to a young man named Ernie. The three of us went to stay at the same time at Auntie and Uncle's house in Lower Wheel Lane. Their house was named "Derwent".

Asked why by Mom, he jokingly said, "Because we derd and went."

At the top of Lower Wheel Lane was a gated cornfield and Uncle walked with me, his little great niece, through it. He showed me how to rub an ear of corn between my hands and blow away the husks. Through the gate at the other side of the field we came out at the back of the Cathedral. The cornfield is no longer there and neither is the open land which has since been built upon. A neighbour's little girl named Joan and I played together. I'd been there almost a week when I felt I could stand it no longer. I felt in the way in the presence of Gwen and Ernie. I cried and asked Uncle to take me home. I was also missing my family, so he gave in to me although I was due to go home the next day. So on the Friday, we made the journey to Coseley on at least three buses. After a rest, dear kind Uncle Isaac made the return journey to Lichfield.

I think it was on this visit to Aunt Rose and Uncle Isaac that he showed me a large book with thick pages made specially to have dried flowers stuck onto them in patterns. It was made in Australia. He said he would give it to me if I would promise to always look after it. I said I would and I've kept my promise. Uncle Isaac is the only man I've ever known who served in the Boer War.

I wanted another bike as I had outgrown the one I'd had from Pauline so Dad had a word with Mr. Davies who owned a bicycle shop in South Street. This street was eventually also covered by Jack Newell Court. He also mended punctures and did all sorts of bicycle repairs. He literally put together a bicycle but when it was completed with its hoop frame, it was too big for me. Before long, Dad sorted out the problem. It went back to Mr. Davis and I was given a new Norman bike. Even now there was a problem: it didn't have a bell.

When Dad came home from the British Legion Club I was always in bed, and for two or three nights when hearing the key in the lock I shouted downstairs, "Have you got the bell Dad?"

Then one night when I asked, came his wordless reply. He just rang the bell.

Whenever my bike had a puncture dad told me to take it to Mr. Davies to be repaired and to say he'd see him in the club. Dad belonged to the British Legion ex Servicemen's Club and this was where he would see Mr. Davies and pay him for mending the puncture. Dad had another friend, Mr. Major Swinnerton who, with his wife, kept a shop at the top of Mason Street on the corner with Oak Street. It is no longer a shop but the building is still there. The Swinnertons had two daughters. Margery was John's age and Gwen was a couple of years older than me. Occasionally they would go in their car and we'd go in ours to somewhere further afield than our regular destinations.

During the school holiday, Dorothy Soden and I went on our bikes to Priory Park, Dudley but when we got there, I was so tired, I went straight back home to bed and slept. Probably the first indication that my thyroid gland didn't work as it should, but it was some years before this was diagnosed.

The time came when my best friend Eileen and I were allowed to go to the Clifton by ourselves. One momentous occasion we went to see Lena Horne in "Stormy Weather", made in 1943. Dad had said I could go if I did my piano practice when I got home. I promised I would and off we went. There we sat in the cheap seats at the front downstairs watching the beautiful Lena Horne singing "Stormy Weather".

I said to Eileen, "Let's watch the film over again so we can watch her sing that again". We did.

I'd remembered my promise and intended to do my piano practice but Dad had had enough. "You can tell Mr. Gill you're not going again," he said, and that was that. I was never destined to play more than one sharp or flat so I was no musical loss to the world.

The Clifton had a Saturday afternoon children's matinée (2d. downstairs, 5d. up) and Eileen and I used to queue to be amused by cartoons, thrilled by cowboys and frightened by whatever the serial was, "Flash Gordon", "Queen of the Jungle", "The Clutching Hand", "The Black Coin" or whatever was running at the time. One Saturday a boy out of our class had been over the Brampits fields picking wild flowers – dog daisies etc. – and he came to the bustling queue for me. I was surprised when I realised who the flowers were for, and me no more than 11. I left the queue to dash across home to put the flowers in water then back again to the queue. The Brampits were the fields now covered by the Bramford Estate.

There were three lads we didn't know who also went to the Saturday afternoon matinée and one day, for a giggle, I said to Eileen, "Let's follow them and find out where they live". So we followed them at a discreet distance, and found out that the particular one we were tracking lived on The Paddock.

A couple of years later when Eileen, Mary Banks and I went to the youth club in Flavell Avenue, we used to dance to records of big band music. There was one boy who jived so well we all watched him in amazement. He was the same lad who lived on The Paddock: Brian Lakin.

Eileen died in August 2004 after years of perfect friendship.

It is said that scarlet fever always leaves its victims with something. With me it was an abscess on the gland in the left side of my neck. Mom had noticed the lump, so took me to see Dr. Waddell who told her she was worrying for nothing. Not happy with this,

Eileen Armstrong (left) and her friend Beryl Moorhouse.

Mom asked Dad to go to see the doctor and say they weren't satisfied with his opinion, so he grudgingly wrote a letter for the specialist Mr. Patrick who I was taken to see the next day.

He was very disturbed and said, "I'll have to have her in right away. If that bursts, it will look as if a dog's bitten her."

The next day, Mom and Dad took me to The Royal Hospital, Wolverhampton, where Mr. Patrick operated and used clips, not stitches, to seal up the long cut. My bed was in the large Dartmouth Ward. I wasn't allowed out of bed for a week at the end of which, my legs were so weak, I had difficulty walking. I'd heard the word, "convalescent", I only knew it meant going somewhere before I went home and sure enough, that's what happened. The place I was taken to was Patshull Hall and lying on my back in the ambulance I could see through the window the overhead wires for the trolleybuses. I later learnt that we'd been going down Tettenhall Road towards Wergs on the way to Patshull. It was a very large house which was in fact a stately home. There were only three beds in the room where I was with two ladies. One was Mrs. Slaney who was a music teacher from Codsall.

The other was much younger, not a great deal older than me being about twenty and in the A.T.S. (Auxiliary Territorial Service). Her name was Kathleen Farmer. Where her home was I have no idea, but I do remember her favourite song was, "My Devotion".

My parents visited me and Mom said, "Well, you always wanted to live in a big house, and now you have."

On the Sunday I went to church with one of the nurses. It was the private church in the grounds of Patshull Hall and to get to it, we had to walk through the large ballroom to get to the wide steps down into the grounds, but what I remember so well were the huge oil paintings on the walls of the ballroom which were covered over. I was told it was because they were pictures of German ancestors. I don't know if this was true or not, but of course, the war was on. The nurse lent me 6d. for the church collection.

Whilst I'd been in hospital, the ones who wanted to take the scholarship had been working hard for the exam. When I returned to school, it was obvious I was far behind the others. Needless to say, I didn't pass to go to Wolverhampton, Dudley nor Bilston High School. It looks like Mom had been right all those years ago about me being born in time to come out of school.

Miss Flavell left school to marry her Dutch airman at the end of term and Eileen and I fulfilled our plans by going to Mrs. Morgan's hardware shop in Castle Street and buying a brown pottery teapot for a half-a-crown (2/6d.) for a wedding present. With it well wrapped and carefully installed in the basket I now had on the front of my bike, we set off to Goldthorn Park Estate where Miss Flavell lived. She was very surprised to see us. She became Mrs. Offers in late 1944.

Two very smartly-dressed ladies in beautiful fur coats came one day, very much to Mom's surprise. The one had been a school friend of Mom's, Grace Cartwright. She had emigrated to Canada years before and the lady with her was a Canadian friend. They lived in Montreal. I asked if they could find me a penfriend as I enjoyed writing and some weeks later I received letters from Nora Shaw and Zina Simonelli. We wrote for years. Nora visited me in 1957, and brought me a gift of a pair of pretty silver earrings. She later married a man named Robert Runciman.

I may have had my love of letter writing from Mom, as she once told me that when she was a girl, she had a penfriend in Africa named Drusilla Josiah, but she kept wanting to be sent things which Nan couldn't afford, so Mom stopped writing.

This wasn't the only visit Mom had from across the Atlantic. There was the occasion when her cousin Hannah Gawlas came with her husband Frank. Hannah's father was Benjamin Smith. He was Nan's eldest brother being older than her by fourteen years. My great uncle Ben had married Keziah Langford from Princes End and around 1911 had emigrated to America taking with them fourteen year old Hannah and seventeen year old Isaac. There were two sons and two daughters older than Isaac. Mom was so pleased to meet Hannah and Frank as she was only nine when her uncle and aunt had emigrated. Hannah was excited at being back in Coseley after so many years and wanted to meet up with all of her cousins.

Mom had tried everything to stop me biting my nails. When I was about eleven she said, "The boys will never look at you if you bite your nails". That did the trick.

My mother still visited Mrs. Fellows wife of Alan, the parents of Sheila who I'd known since pram days. Mrs. Fellows told Mom that Sheila who had attended The Manor Junior School was now going to a private school in Wolverhampton called Ely House Ladies' College on the Tettenhall Road. I liked the idea and asked Dad if he would let me go there. After much discussion, it was agreed that I could go if I was accepted by the Principals who were sisters – the Misses Jenkins who were as different as chalk and cheese. Miss Jenkins was the eldest, and wore a blue Harris tweed suit and her sister was called Miss Amy, and she wore a long black dress. After an interview I was accepted and before the beginning of the next term, Mom and I went to Green & Hollins outfitters in Queen's Square, Wolverhampton to get my new school uniform, colours were light blue and navy blue.

Chapter 8

The next term I caught the Midland Red bus to Wolverhampton then the Green Corporation trolleybus from outside the Grand Theatre to Chapel Ash at the cost of a ha'penny (½d). The fare on the other bus was 3½d from Roseville to town. I now travelled for the first time on a trolleybus courtesy of the overhead cables I had seen through the ambulance window on my way to Patshull Hall. The school fee each term was 10 gns. guineas (£10.10s.0d.) which we had to take with us in an envelope and drop it into a basket held by Miss Amy who was there to meet us at the back door. Like all the other girls, I was dressed in my gym slip, blouse and tie, blazer and hat with its distinctive band and badge, the same as the one on my blazer, only smaller. I loved my uniform and wore it with pride. I was told to go to the top floor to Class 4c. Eventually, the bell rang and everyone dashed to go downstairs to the gym where the assembly was held. The spiral stairs to the floor below were awful and I was on the narrow edge. My heel slipped and I bounced painfully down almost to the bottom. What a thing to happen on my first day in front of so many strangers!

Sheila, being 6 months older than me, was in Class 4b, but I soon made friends particularly with Jean Baker and Margaret Gater. I was soon to have lessons in Latin, French, algebra and geometry which would not have happened at Mount Pleasant School, not that I ever shone in any of these subjects, but I did enjoy geography, history and English and always liked writing composition. We read "Alice in Wonderland" for English literature and had to buy our own copies. I saw a beautiful linen-bound copy in the newsagents on the Birmingham New Road in Coseley. It had in it lovely black and white scenes from the film. The price was half-a-crown (2/6d.), and my parents let me buy it. Mom had taught me years before how to cover books with brown paper, so I covered all my school books.

There were two teachers who were also sisters and fiercely Welsh: Mrs. Gundy and Mrs. Kidson. Mrs. Kidson was by far the nicer of the two. Another teacher was Mrs. Palmer. It was she who took us for French and music. I still think of her every time I hear Elgar's Pomp and Circumstance March as we were taught it with patriotic words. The Jenkins' cat was named Marmalade for obvious reasons and although we were three stories high, he would sometimes sit on the window ledge, having jumped first onto the conservatory roof. Ely House was an imposing Georgian building with an enormous bay window to the right side of the centre front door. It had been a girls' school for decades, but also took boys to the age of five.

My cousin Bob had left Wolverhampton Grammar School when I started Ely House and I was given his leather satchel complete with stretched bulges made by the reinforced toecaps of his football boots which had kept company with his books going to Wolverhampton since he was eleven.

Ely House School, now Ely House Hotel. By kind permission of Ken Anwar.

One day, I was standing at the bus stop opposite the Art Gallery, happily eating an ice cream and waiting for the number one bus to go back to school after lunch when a fifth-former came up to me and said, "If Jenks sees you eating that, she'll go mad." I finished it quickly. After all, Ely House was a ladies' college.

Sometimes, I'd go home for lunch, but I had to leave class early in order to get back for the afternoon. On reflection, it was foolhardy to do this midday as it was such a rush.

When I took sandwiches instead, Mom always reminded me, "Bring the bag back." Because of the paper shortage, we looked after our lunch bags. No plastic then.

At the same time that I was at Ely House, a friend of mine named Hazel Fones was attending the Queen's Business College in Lich Gates, Wolverhampton near to St. Peter's Collegiate Church. She left there later than I left school and some days I waited for her, sitting on the step of the college so we could come home on the same bus. Mom said there was a Fones family

Left: Sheila Fellows and me on the park, 9th May 1948. Right: With my cousin, Vera.

connection, but it wasn't until years later that I discovered that Hazel was my third cousin. We shared our Fones' great-great-grandparents.

It was Tuesday 16th May 1944 and John came to meet me from school to stop me going home. He told me Nan had died and he wanted to stop me from going home as Mom was so upset. We went for a walk. Nan had been ill for sometime, and her bed had been downstairs. The nurse, Sister Lawton, had been coming in most days. Uncle Albert and Uncle Will had been coming to stay, taking turns to help Mom when they could and would stay the night. I wasn't aware at the time, but it must have been Saturday nights when they stayed because of them going to work. Some nights during school holidays, I was allowed to stay the night with my cousin Rita, Uncle Harry's daughter, and other nights with my cousin Vera, Uncle Will's daughter. When we were younger, Vera and I were taken to Miss Rea and Miss Roberts; size-wise the Laurel and Hardy respectively of the tailoressing business in Lord Street, Bradley where Vera and I were measured and had made beautiful Harris tweed coats and matching hats.

My brother began having ballroom dancing lessons around 1944 at the Conservative Club in Dudley. He used to come home, roll back the rugs, put a record on the record player and practise with me which was good. This was how I learnt to dance without actually being taught. At about this time, John being 16, joined the A.T.C. The war was still raging and lots of youths joined the Air Training Corps. It helped them for when they were called up to join the forces, be it Air Force, Army or Navy. The A.T.C. met and trained in the hall of Mount Pleasant School. They also had dances some Saturday nights, and the G.T.C. (Girls' Training Corps) went along to partner the boys. John being a pianist used to play piano for the dances alternate weeks with Harold Rich. Much as I wanted to join the G.T.C. I wasn't old enough and by the time I was, the war, thankfully, was over.

My brother became a teacher. After being at three or four schools in the Black Country, he went to teach Forces' children in Germany, taking his wife Norma and two little sons Andrew and David. He first taught at Osnabrück then Sennelager and lastly Detmold before returning to England to be headmaster of Metheringham Primary School in Lincolnshire. He wrote music for the school plays and pantomimes. Living in Cranwell, he soon became involved with the Cranwell Singers and theatre group at the prestigious R.A.F. College, his reputation having preceded him. Before leaving England, as well as teaching, John was architect and builder of six houses including his own on The Paddock. He wasn't short of talent.

At church there was to be a play. A very pretty girl about three years older than me was chosen to play Mary Magdalene. The girl said "Trust them to choose me to play a prostitute". Whatever was a prostitute?

Aunt Eva was never well, and suffered severely from asthma. She died towards the end of 1944, leaving Uncle Albert and Bob on their own at their home in Langley Avenue. By this time Bill was abroad in the R.A.F. and Bob was a Bevin Boy in the mines, later serving on board the Royal Navy aircraft carrier H.M.S. Theseus. Mom was very fond of Auntie Eva, and she was with her when she died.

When my cousin Albert was older, he went into the theatre, changing his name to Robert Patrick. He would have kept his own surname, but there was already an actor, very well known, named Robert Newton. He was in Reading, Shrewsbury and Wednesbury Repertory Companies. I saw him at Shrewsbury in the comedy, "See How They Run". He was brilliant and just as good in drama. He had to leave the stage due to ill health. He would have gone far. There were several well-known actors he counted amongst his friends, including Donald Pleasance. He was an accomplished painter in oils and watercolours and when in the theatre he also painted scenery. After this time he would answer only to

My cousins, Bill Newton and his brother Bob.

the name Bob, but he was officially R.P.A. Newton. He later went into teaching, and was known as Mr. Newton, becoming a lecturer at Wednesbury College, and became very involved in the Walsall Artist Society, also teaching at Lichfield College. He did a lot of work for Mencap in Walsall, teaching art.

For Christmas 1944, my parents gave me the first publication of the "Film Review" by F. Maurice Speed. It was the first of his many such annuals which were excellent and in due course gave me hours and hours of pleasure. I was charmed by Frank Sinatra and Bing Crosby from the first time I saw and heard them and that charm has never faded so I was doubly delighted years later when I saw "High Society" (1956) with the icing on the

Robert Patrick Albert Newton.

cake, Louis Armstrong. It was because of seeing the musical films that I fell in love with big band music. What some might call a misspent youth formed my life-long love of music. My Dad loved music. His favourites were the operettas "The New Moon", "The Maid of the Mountains" and "The Desert Song". He enjoyed other kinds of music as well, just as I like all kinds including Gilbert and Sullivan, but most of all Traditional Jazz. I was surprised on the occasion we went to see "Sentimental Journey" (1946) and I realised he was silently crying. It was tenderness that made him do that and fairness that made him pay workmen the same as he paid himself for doing the same job and it was care and consideration that led him to ask Horace Smout to deliver a bag of logs to a recent war widow when her sailor husband was lost at sea. This to be done anonymously and logs, as coal was rationed.

One day I went home from school and told Mom something unbelievable. "Rose Ruddick says they can get hot water without having a fire". This of course referred to an immersion heater, something that was new and up to now unheard of by my Mom and Dad.

Our house and all others like it had been built with a copper in the corner of the kitchen which every Monday morning was filled with cold water and a fire lit in the grate beneath it. When the water was boiling the weekly wash would be done. Little wonder that my mother thought it impossible get hot water at the flick of a switch. Nothing short of a miracle. Further to this, Mom had a friend named Elsie Phillips who was the sister of Mrs. Dorothy Jones, Beryl's mom. Elsie married a man named Tom Shipley who was in the family business which made tiled fire grates. The showroom was in Chapel Ash, Wolverhampton. This led to Mom and Dad deciding to have our grate taken out and replaced by a beautiful tiled one which meant the boiler was taken out and put in the bathroom, so we now had an immersion heater like Rose's mom and dad. Because we lived in a council house, I suppose Dad had to get permission from the council to do this.

The parents of one of my school friends invited me to their home to stay one weekend. They were Mr and Mrs. Baker and they kept the "Butcher's Arms" in Willenhall. I always enjoyed being with Jean.

There was one day at Ely House that was extra special. For several days the Misses Jenkins had been taking it in turns to listen to the radio waiting for a very special announcement. Then one day Miss Amy came excitedly into the class room and said, "You can all go home. The war's over". It was Tuesday 8th May, 1945.

We did all go home that day but the war wasn't entirely over. Fighting was still raging in the Far East and continued until victory over Japan was declared on 15th August the same year.

On Thursday, 5th July 1945, the day of the General Election, Father Bourne came to see Mom. He said to her, "Emily, have you been to vote yet?" "Not yet Father," she answered. "You must, Emily, you must. I'm not going to tell you who to vote for, but if we don't get Mr. Churchill in, it will be a catastrophe." Winston Churchill didn't become Prime Minister on that occasion, but he did when the next General Election took place in 1951.

Mrs. Bourne was a very sweet lady, but unusual, as she was known to take her knitting with her when they occasionally went to the Clifton.

As Mom had been a shorthand typist, having my future in mind, she suggested I have lessons from a lady who lived in the village. She was Miss Elsie Blewitt who was a second cousin of Mom's and during some evenings had pupils at her home in Avenue Road. I tried but was just no good at it. I learnt the signs for the consonants and vowels but could never think quickly enough whether the outline should go above, on or through the line, whether they should be light or dark pencil strokes or should I make an upward or downward "r". What a disappointment I must have been to Mom and as for touch-typing! It was all asking too much.

My Cousin Vera also went to Elsie Blewitt's and eventually used her shorthand and typing skills in her job in the Cannon offices. Vera's sister, my cousin Joan, became a probationary nurse at Shifnal Cottage Hospital. She became a State Registered Nurse and went to work at Southampton General Hospital where she nursed a patient who she eventually married and they still live in Southampton.

By the time I was about twelve, I'd had enough of my straight hair and persuaded Mom to let me have a perm. The hairdresser I went to was in Swan Village. It was a small, one-storey, building which originally was a toll house situated on Sedgley Road West. This same building was one of the lucky old buildings as it was transported and rebuilt at the Black Country Living Museum. The perm was a Callinan, unusual because the customer wasn't connected up to a perming machine.

The following year Miss Jenkins and Miss Amy surprised us all by saying they were going to retire, then the news went around that another teacher, Mrs. Shaw, was almost certainly going to take over the school. The two teachers who were sisters had made it known they would be leaving and intended to start a school of their own in a house in Wolverhampton Road East. It was a stylish building in a terrace of houses and was to be called Tudor House School. Well what else! After all they were Welsh.

Although I didn't like Mrs. Gundy, I thought I'd like to go there because I preferred Mrs. Kidson to Mrs. Shaw. Tudor House was to open in January 1947. So it was arranged that I should go there along with a few more of the girls when the time came.

There was a girl named Jean Calvert who was a friend of John and Bob. She often came to our house and she talked about having singing lessons from Mr. Ingram at Tividale. I enjoyed singing and thought lessons would help me to be better at it, so asked Dad. Mom took me to see Mr. Ingram. I sang for him and he agreed to take me.

It was the 22nd June 1946 when my cousin Bill married Nell (Ellen) Wall at St. Chad's church. Bill's brother Bob was unable to be best man as he was in the Royal Navy and abroad at the time. Bill was in the Royal Air Force and he asked my brother who was also in the R.A.F. Both bridegroom and best man wore their R.A.F. uniform for the occasion and both blancoed their webbing belt. This was against King's Regulations. I've never heard if they were reprimanded, but they looked very smart on the photographs. It must have seemed strange to the wedding guests because on that same day, the new east window was covered with blackout material as it was due to be unveiled that afternoon by the Bishop of Shrewsbury along with a

Bill and Nell Newton.

memorial plaque with the names of twenty-two service men of the parish who lost their lives in the Second World War. The window and plaque were paid for with subscriptions from parishioners.

When the Bournes eventually left St. Chad's in the Spring of 1948, they moved to St. Stephen's church, Wolverhampton. In the Summer, St. Chad's Mothers' Union had a coach trip to visit them. Mom, seeing that the vicar was absolutely glowing said, "Oh, father, you do look well," and referring to the pungent smell coming from the nearby Springfield brewery he replied, "It's the hops, Emily, it's the hops."

I was now thirteen and my confirmation was scheduled to take place on Sunday 13th October 1946. A group of us had had lessons and been drilled in the catechism by the vicar, Father Bourne. Mom and I both wanted Dad to be there and finally he agreed to come to church that day. They gave me a gold cross and chain to mark the occasion. I wore a white dress and veil and a pair of tan-coloured wedge heel lace-up shoes. Doreen Hughes and I knelt together as we were confirmed by the Bishop of Stafford.

It was Bonfire Night and I went to the bonfire in Wilson Road. Alice Webb, the eldest of the Webb family, was cooking gray peas, and jacket potatoes were being cooked in the bonfire. It was great. One of the lads I knew said, "Let's go round and look at the bonfires," so we set off. It was early evening and in Old Meeting Road we met Dad going home.

"Hello Dad. We're just going to see the bonfires."

"All right," he said, "Mind what you're doing."

Just two weeks later, Mom was going to the Clifton with her friend Ada to see Bing Crosby in, "Going My Way". Mrs. Siviter arrived ready to go to the pictures and the three of us were going together, but Mom said she wouldn't go until Dad came home from work.

Anxious to go, I was watching for him through the back window and when I saw him shouted "Dad's here!" Seconds later, he took one step into the house and collapsed. Somehow, Mom and Mrs. Siviter got him onto the settee. Mom rang for the doctor, but within a few minutes Dad died. It was Tuesday 19th November 1946 and Dad was only 46 years old.

By this time, my brother was in the R.A.F. doing two years National Service. Mom rang the R.A.F. Camp in Gloucester where he was stationed and compassionate leave was arranged.

Mom thought it had been prophetic that Dad had said to John before he went back to camp on Sunday, "Come and have a walk with me for the last time."

Mom didn't want me to go to the funeral so I was taken by her old friend, Mrs. Dorothy Jones, to the Grand Theatre, Wolverhampton to see a play but I've no recollection what we saw.

John had been given an overseas posting but when he applied to stay in this country due to the change of family circumstances, it was granted. In fact, he was transferred to Cosford which was a home posting. He used to travel there every day by coach which he caught by the park gates.

Singing lessons never started.

Life, without Dad, would never be the same again.

Cpl. John Alfred Hyde, in R.A.F. Uniform.

Chapter 9

The Winter of 1947 was one of the worst in living memory. I was having difficulty walking as I had several verrucas on my foot. So bad were they, I had to go to Dudley Guest Hospital and have an operation to have them removed. The one had grown in so deeply, I had to have a stitch in the ball of my foot. With Dad no longer around, Uncle Harry fetched me home from the hospital. I wasn't away overnight. It meant being away from school for a week, but I still had the stitch in my foot when I went back in that awful weather. That Winter was dreadful.

Changing my navy blue and light blue for red, I started school at Tudor House after Christmas but then I began to realise what paying school fees would mean to Mom, so I told her I would leave school at the end of term and get a job if it would help. She said it would, so in due course she wrote to the Heads who naturally knew about my Dad. At this time, pupils were allowed to leave school at 14. I took the letter and gave it to Mrs. Gundy. She sent a letter to Mom which I, in fact, still have. It was a very hurtful letter and upset Mom greatly. Mrs. Gundy said she wouldn't have accepted me at the school had she known I would leave so soon. There was no word of sympathy for my recently bereaved mother.

Mom was only 44 when we lost Dad and she knew she needed to get a job: she needed the money.

Shortly before I left school, I saw the most beautiful pair of Joyce shoes in the window of Craddocks shop in Dudley Street, Wolverhampton. The sight of them drew me like a magnet. They were flat shoes with wedge heels and platform soles. The heels and platform were in champagne-coloured leather, and the uppers the same colour suede, apron fronts and four-hole lace up. They were just beautiful, but so expensive. After all, they were Joyce, an American make. How could I possibly persuade Mom to meet me out of school to see them and how could I expect to have them? They were 4gns. (four pounds and four shillings). This was more money than a lot of people earned in a week. I told Mom about them, and begged her to just come and look at them. She did, and I still don't think I'd ever done anything to deserve them but she bought them for me. Perhaps she thought that as we'd lost Dad, I ought to have a treat to cheer me up. I shall never know.

When Mom left school at the age of 14 she started work at Hedge's shoe factory in Bilston, doing the lowliest of jobs: cutting off the cottons on the shoe uppers which were taken to her in large boxes. It was a soul destroying job and she told me that from her work bench she could see the birds outside and she thought to herself that she wished she was a bird and could fly away. She told this to Nan so she paid for Mom to go to Gripton's Business College which was in Dudley opposite St. Edmund's church and there she learned the skill of shorthand, typing and book keeping. When she left she became a shorthand typist at Wright's Forge and Engineering in Sedgley Road West, Tipton. There she had made friends with Miss Edith Richards, whose home was in Fraser Street Bilston. It became a life-long friendship, and I called the lady Auntie Edith. There was a vacancy for a shorthand typist at Beacon Machine Tools, Hurst Lane, Tipton for which she applied, and was offered the job. I was at home when she got back from the interview and she cried. She'd been offered £3.10.0d a week and she said she'd never earned so much money before. Dad had never kept her short. He had always been generous.

I had no idea what I wanted to do for a job. Mom suggested I should train to be a comptometer operator like Joan Millinson. I was filled with horror at the thought of anything to do with arithmetic, as it was a subject I hated. Then Mom had an idea. She would speak to Frank Morris, who with his brother, owned the Victoria Printing Company in Queens Road, Tipton where Dad had had the business printing done. An appointment was made for us to see Mr. Morris. I was to train to become a bookbinder. I should have to use a large, foot-operated perforator, a hand-operated numbering machine, collate different-coloured printed paper into sets to be used with carbon paper and pack up stationery orders for customers.

I met Mr. Dunn and Mr. Shayler who were the ones who used the printing machines, Jack Williams who used the big, lethal guillotine to cut paper to the required size for different jobs and Mr. Crewe who was the typesetter. Later Mr. Crew told me that when he was a boy in the Scouts he went to the top of Sedgley

Beacon and had seen the sun shining on the Bristol Channel.

My domestic chore would be to make tea and wash up twice a day. The lady who would be my teacher and trainer was at the time on honeymoon and when she came back to work I knew her to be Mrs. Kathleen Coulson. Mom talked wages to Mr. Morris and he said 17/- (seventeen shillings) a week.

Mom said, "Could you make it seventeen and six?" to which he agreed.

The seventeen and six turned out to be seventeen and tuppence (17/2d.) as fourpence was deducted for tax. Out of this Mom gave me half-a-crown a week. I left school on Friday 11th April, 1947 and started work the following Monday.

My adult life had begun.

Claudia aged 16. Photo taken by Roy Hipkins whose cousin Norma Johnson married John Hyde in 1956.

Maternal Family Tree

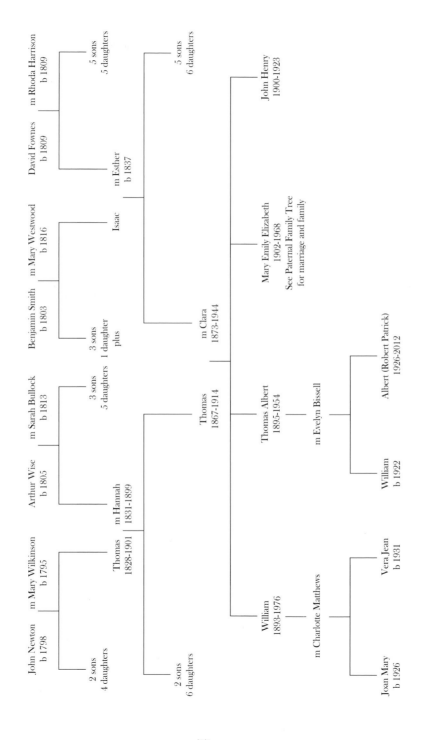

John Newton
b 1798

m Mary Wilkinson
b 1795

2 sons
4 daughters

Arthur Wise
b 1805

m Sarah Bullock
b 1813

3 sons
5 daughters

Benjamin Smith
b 1803

m Mary Westwood
b 1816

3 sons
1 daughter
plus

Isaac

David Fownes
b 1809

m Rhoda Harrison
b 1809

5 sons
5 daughters

m Esther
b 1837

5 sons
6 daughters

Thomas
1828-1901

m Hannah
1831-1899

2 sons
6 daughters

Thomas
1867-1914

m Clara
1873-1944

William
1893-1976

m Charlotte Matthews

Thomas Albert
1895-1954

m Evelyn Bissell

Mary Emily Elizabeth
1902-1968
See Paternal Family Tree
for marriage and family

John Henry
1900-1923

Joan Mary
b 1926

Vera Jean
b 1931

William
b 1922

Albert (Robert Patrick)
1926-2012

Paternal Family Tree

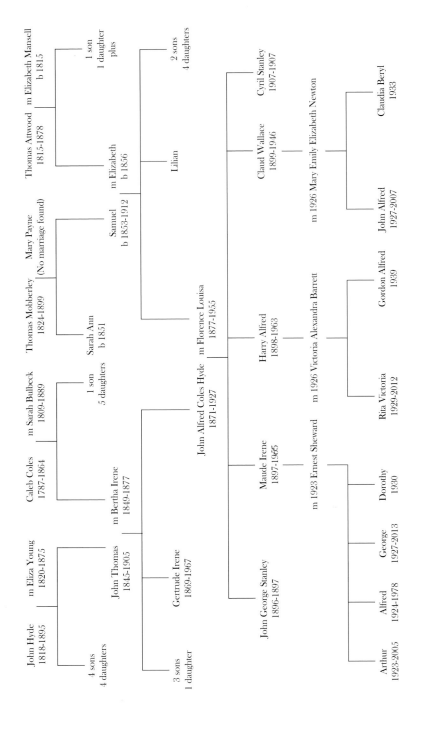